INTERPRETING THE BIBLE

Issues in Religious Studies

GENERAL EDITORS
Professor Peter Baelz and Jean Holm

Further titles in this series

INTERPRETING THE BIBLE

David Stacey

SHELDON PRESS
LONDON

First published in Great Britain in 1976 by
Sheldon Press, Marylebone Road, London NW1 4DU

Third impression 1983

Copyright © 1976 David Stacey

Printed in Great Britain by
Biddles Ltd, Guildford, Surrey

ISBN 0 85969 091 1

CONTENTS

DAVID STACEY was born in Bristol and educated there at Queen Elizabeth's Hospital and at Birmingham University. He entered the Methodist ministry and has been a teacher and lecturer in biblical studies for more than twenty years. He is a member of the Society for Old Testament Study. He now teaches and lives in Cambridge. He is married with three grown up children.

Issues in Religious Studies

GENERAL PREFACE TO THE SERIES

This series of books offers an introduction to some of the central issues involved in religious studies. It aims to be as dispassionate as possible, assuming a serious interest on the part of the reader but neither previous study in the area nor commitment to any religious position. It seeks to combine a basic rigour of thought with a concreteness of approach.

The purpose of each book is to indicate the nature of the issue, the questions raised by it, and the main directions in which thinkers have looked for answers to such questions. It should thus provide a firm foundation on which further study can be built.

The series was designed in the first place to meet the needs of students embarking on courses in religious studies in colleges of education and universities, and of senior pupils following the revised 'A' level syllabuses. However, the books are not in any narrow sense 'text books', and it is hoped that they will be of value to anyone approaching a study of these issues for the first time.

Peter Baelz and Jean Holm

Part 1

ISSUES

1

INTRODUCTION

Buying a Bible is a complicated exercise, because Bibles come in so many forms. There are leatherbound volumes to be read in the pulpit, cheap paperbacks to be read on the train, meticulous translations to satisfy the scholar, simple translations for those whose English is poor, annotated editions, illustrated, abbreviated editions, A crop of initials has sprouted in the catalogues—AV, RV, RSV, NEB, JB, TEV, and so on.[1]

Giving the Bible to everyone is not a new idea. When Erasmus published his Greek New Testament in 1516, he wrote in the preface, 'I totally disagree with those who are unwilling that the Holy Scriptures, translated into the common tongue, should be read by the unlearned ... I wish that the farm worker might sing parts of them at the plough, that the weaver might hum them at the shuttle, and that the traveller might beguile the weariness of the way by reciting them.'[2]

In Erasmus' day printing was difficult, and it took some time for his wish to be fulfilled. In England the publication of the Authorized Version in 1611 was the critical breakthrough. This work—little short of a miracle, for it was the product of a commission—remained unchallenged for centuries. Then, with the Revised Versions of 1881 (Britain) and 1901 (U.S.A.), things began to change. The one Bible, which belonged firmly in the Church, began to give way to different Bibles, some of which were never meant for reading in church or in public at all. In the last few decades there has been a flood of Bibles, and Erasmus' wish has been fulfilled beyond his wildest expectation.

---

[1] Authorized Version 1611, Revised Version 1881 and 1885, Revised Standard Version 1946 and 1952, New English Bible 1961 and 1970, Jerusalem Bible 1966, Today's English Version 1966.

[2] See F. F. Bruce, *The English Bible* (Lutterworth 1961), p. 29.

3

One might well ask why there were some in Erasmus' day who were unwilling that the Scriptures should be read by the unlearned. The answer is twofold. In the first place, it was argued that the Scriptures were the Word of God, mysterious and beyond price, and, therefore, beyond the understanding of peasants. In the second place, it was argued that God in his wisdom had established a Church with doctors, bishops and priests to whom the responsibility of expounding the Scriptures was given. The peasant had best learn his Bible from them. If he read it for himself he would go wrong.

These arguments appear now to have been abandoned by everybody. There is universal agreement that the Bible should be widely read, that the simple will not be confused, that lack of scholarship will not prove an impossible handicap.

If this is so, why do we need a book on interpretation? Because the Bible, in common with all great works of art and literature, can be appreciated or understood at many different levels. First acquaintance may be illuminating, but the range and depth of the Bible's teaching come into view only when the text is studied with the help of linguistic, literary and historical techniques, and the philosophical problems raised by the deceptively simple phrase 'the Bible's teaching' have been sorted out. The present book attempts to summarize the issues involved.

The best way to begin is by raising the question of how meaning relates to a text. There are two directions in which we can look for meaning. On the one hand, there is the intention of the author; on the other, the meaning his readers grasp from the text. In theory these two coincide, but in practice different readers grasp different things and no reader grasps exactly what the author meant to express. On the simplest level meaning intended and meaning grasped are so close that there are no problems, but, in more complicated areas, doubts and uncertainties arise. Compare the message, 'I will see you under the clock at five on Thursday', with the politician's statement, 'We are on the brink of a major crisis'. In one case, meaning intended and meaning grasped will be identical. In the other, columns in the press may not exhaust all the possible implications and innuendoes.

As far as the Bible is concerned there are several complicating factors that make even the politician's speech an unsatisfactory analogy. In the first place, with regard to the Bible one cannot speak of a single author and a single intent. The book of Genesis is a collection of traditions preserved in oral form for centuries, later written down and several times edited. On a lesser scale the same is true of Mark's Gospel. Sayings of Jesus and stories about him were remembered, collected and edited over several decades. The final redactor put his stamp on them, but no single person gave us Mark's Gospel.[3] When the facts of authorship are complicated, the problems regarding meaning intended are intensified.

In the second place, the Bible belongs to a culture to which we are strangers, it came into being in an age far removed from ours in time, and it was written in languages that few of us have mastered. All translation means interpretation, and where the gap of culture, time and language is great, the element of interpretation may be considerable. There is no way round this. Ancient Hebrew expresses the idea of, shall we say, personal identity in its own peculiar terms and with reference to a social structure that has long since vanished. For us the idea has to be expressed in English and in relation to different experience of society. In such circumstances precision is hardly to be expected.

In the third place, the Bible makes constant use of oblique forms of discourse—symbol, parable, allegory, myth—a realm in which sharp definitions do not exist and where complete identity between meaning intended and meaning grasped is impossible. There is a difference between a navigator's chart and a novel. One gives bearings and distances, the other explores attitudes and relationships. Meaning in the case of the novel is more elusive than meaning in the case of the chart. Interpreting the Bible similarly calls not only for knowledge and skill but for imaginative subtlety as well.

There is a fourth factor that takes us right to the heart of the problem. A distinction must be drawn between the original

[3] The redactor is the technical name given to the person who was responsible for the final stage of each of the Synoptic Gospels. In the past it has been assumed that the redactor's responsibility was small, that he simply tidied up the collections of material that were transmitted to him. Today, however, the redactor is regarded as a creative person who, by selection and arrangement of material, put his own positive stamp on the Gospel, thereby investing it with the theology of the particular community to which he belonged.

meaning of passages in the Bible and the meaning they have for today. With care and skill a scholar might be able to say what the book of Amos meant to eighth-century Israel, but modern students of the Bible look for meaning of a different kind. For them it is not simply a matter of Amos and Israel, but also of God and mankind. So both the elements in meaning are suddenly and dramatically expanded. In the work of Amos and his editors the modern reader looks for words with more than human authority, and in place of the original hearers and readers he puts himself, his own religious communion and, indeed, all mankind.

It is also necessary to remember that modern students of the Bible have very different backgrounds. Jews, Catholics, Protestants, Jehovah's Witnesses and many others search the Bible for present guidance. While disagreeing about the contemporary significance of particular passages, they are united in the view that the distinction between original sense and modern sense is a real one. This distinction is so important that it is proper to speak of two separate techniques in the field of biblical studies, one concerned with original meaning and commonly called *exegesis*, the other concerned with present meaning and sometimes called *hermeneutics*. The terms are not always used strictly, and there is the third term, 'interpretation', that may mean both undertakings or, alternatively, may be used as a less technical name for the second. We shall use the words exegesis and interpretation consistently to refer to the two tasks.

Exegesis is necessary with all ancient books. Our appreciation of Chaucer is enriched by those who have some knowledge of fourteenth-century England and who, by means of footnotes, bring out subtle points that would otherwise be lost. Similarly we need exegesis of the Bible. The work covers a wide field. The exegete has to be familiar with textual studies so that he can know what the original version probably was; he must be familiar with styles, forms, categories of writing, so that he can classify passages and draw conclusions about their function; he must be a good linguist to appreciate the nuances of the original; he must understand the ancient situations so that historical allusions will not be lost on him; he must be able to recognize the slant of the various editors who have worked over the text. Exegetical commentaries represent a sophisticated form of biblical scholarship.

A simple example of the value of exegesis is provided by the parable of the Good Samaritan, where the point is made more clear if one realizes who the Samaritans were and why the Jews despised them. A more complex problem is presented by the enigmatic words of Mark 8.31, 'the Son of Man must suffer many things'. Did Jesus speak of himself in this way? What is the point of the 'Son of Man' designation? What is the significance of the suffering of the Son of Man? Such questions are not easy, and the deeper the exegete probes, the more intractable they become.

Biblical exegetes are usually theologians of one kind or another, but the work can be carried out by one whose interest is purely historical. No presuppositions about the continuing religious importance of the Bible today are necessary.

All exegesis is grist to the interpreter's mill, but interpretation is a separate undertaking. The interpreter takes his stand on the belief that the Bible is not simply the product of human inventiveness, that over and beyond the overt intent of the writers there is a deeper intent not always understood by the writers themselves and that consequently the Bible has some kind of universal relevance.

An example of interpretation is to be seen in the application of some of Paul's ethical exhortations to the modern world. The exegete can explain why Paul appealed to Philemon in the terms that he did; the interpreter tries to translate that appeal into an attitude and a mode of conduct that are applicable today. A more complicated example comes from the world of Christology.[4] Many titles are applied to Jesus, either directly or by implication, in the New Testament. The exegete makes clear what is being asserted in each case, but the question that Christians have to decide is what it all means in terms of Christ's essential nature and how that can be communicated in the twentieth century. That is a matter of interpretation.

All this does not mean that Erasmus was wrong. There is a

[4] Christology is the area of Christian theology which has to do with the person of Jesus Christ. The problems of describing one who is held to be both God and man are manifold, and Christians have been accused of contradictions and confusions from the beginning. Christology is the attempt of Christians to put forward a coherent account of the mystery of the incarnation.

7

sense, even an authority, in the Bible exactly as it stands. But no religious group that values learning can be satisfied with the ploughboy's understanding. Through its scholars it must probe deeper. It must unravel the mysteries of the ancient text and put forward hypotheses concerning its relevance from generation to generation.

2

CONTEXT AND POINT OF VIEW

The process of interpretation implies two elements, a source to be interpreted and a human subject who is the interpreter. In this chapter we are more concerned with the human subject than with the Bible itself.

This approach may alarm those readers who affirm that the Bible is the Word of God, that it must be allowed to speak for itself and that the human subject, if given too much scope, will obscure the divine Word. This attitude seems reasonable, but the interpreter cannot be disposed of altogether. The Bible cannot speak for itself. Someone must open it, select a passage, read and draw conclusions. It is possible to surround this circumstance with various theological contentions; it may be said that the reader was guided in his selection, that his reading and understanding were enlightened, and so on. But it remains that there is a human subject involved. The Bible cannot be the Word of God in a vacuum.

If the interpreter stands within one of the great religious traditions, that tradition will determine what version of the Bible he reads. This is not a matter of translation but of contents. For the Jew, the Torah, the Prophets and the Writings constitute the sacred Scriptures.[1] Profound and significant interpretations of the Torah have been made within Judaism, but they cannot easily be transferred to other contexts where different versions of Scripture are venerated.

Until recent years there were differences about contents within

[1] The Torah, the supreme document of Judaism, is the first five books of the Old Testament. The word is impossible to translate. 'Law' is not adequate. 'Direction' or 'instruction' is a little better. The Prophets include Joshua, Judges, 1 and 2 Samuel and 1 and 2 Kings, as well as the more obvious prophetic books. The Writings contain much diverse material including Psalms, Job and Proverbs. See below pp. 50f.

the Christian tradition. The Reformers expressed doubts about some of the Old Testament books, particularly those which appeared in the longer, Greek Old Testament but not in the Hebrew. Roman Catholic Bibles never faltered, for they were related to Jerome's Vulgate, which followed the Greek. Protestant leaders made use of a number of devices to reduce in importance those books that came from the Greek but were not in the Hebrew. In the Authorized Version they became the Apocrypha. For many years the Apocrypha was left out of English Bibles, and many serious works of interpretation were written which paid no heed to it at all.

All this is now largely a matter of history. In these days of ecumenical panels, arguments about the constitution of the canon have died away. None the less the example shows that the context from which the interpreter begins his work may determine the very definition of the Bible on which he works.

The context is important in other ways. Every religious body develops its own attitudes, presuppositions and doctrines. Baptists, for example, have a clear idea who should be baptized. Other Christian bodies have different ideas, yet all would claim that Scripture supports their own confessional view. How does it come about that Baptist interpreters consistently read the evidence one way and, say, Methodists read it another?

The answer must be that the modern Baptist scholar is heir to a theological tradition that has developed a coherent body of doctrine within which believers' baptism is fully integrated. The Methodist scholar is heir to a divergent, but equally coherent, tradition. No interpreter can rid himself of ideas and impressions received from his tradition, even supposing he wished to. No interpreter can go to the Bible without presuppositions. It is not surprising, therefore that the Baptist continues to find scriptural evidence to confirm him in his view and the Methodist finds the opposite.

This is not to suggest that scholarship is simply a matter of confirming traditions. Scholars play their part in criticizing notions received from the past, and from time to time interpreters produce theses of startling novelty that cannot be traced back to any pre-existing context or influence. Joseph Smith, Charles Taze Russell and Mary Baker Eddy, founders of the Mormon Church, the Jehovah's Witnesses and Christian Science, respectively, are three nineteenth-century examples. The context of the interpreter is not everything, but it cannot be ignored.

Apart from the confessional context, the interpreter has a historical context. Both he and the people he addresses live under the strains and stresses of a particular decade. Every period has a mood which shows itself in art, literature, fashion, diet, humour, indeed in all things human. Theology is not insensitive to it. In the positive optimistic years of the nineteenth century, when cultivated Europeans were so much impressed with their own achievements, it was not too difficult to see the Christian faith as the inspiration that was guiding men towards the Utopia which the Scriptures seemed to speak of as the Kingdom of God. But when Karl Barth sat down to write his 'Commentary on the Epistle to the Romans' almost within sound of the guns on the western front, no such hopes were possible. Life was not good at Verdun or Passchendaele, and human achievement seemed diabolical rather than impressive.

The interpreter is not overruled by his decade any more than by his confessional tradition, but he will find that some passages in the Bible speak to his age with a peculiar aptness. These may well provide his themes. If the purpose of interpretation is to apply the Scriptures to the life and thought of a particular community or individual, the circumstances of the recipients cannot be overlooked.

Finally we come to the interpreter himself. Whatever kind of man he is, he will have beliefs, characteristics, attitudes and a personal history that mark him as an individual. His method is not as subjective as that of the painter, to whom personal impressions are all-important, but neither is it as objective as that of the scientist, who, in proving his hypothesis, tries hard to eliminate any factor which might derive from himself as the observer. The interpreter stands under the discipline of his material, but he must work on it as a person.

As a person he does not stand still. He learns and grows. In one way the interpreter and the scientist are similar, for both begin with tentative hypotheses and are ready to abandon them if they fail to work out. The interpreter who studies the Bible is unlikely to find that his first efforts provide an 'open sesame' to biblical truth. He must try again and again, recognizing that he is being instructed by the Bible all the time. In this way a relationship builds up between the interpreter and his material, faith interpreting Bible and Bible informing faith. Perhaps the worst mistake any interpreter can make is to begin with a rigid hypothesis and to press on with it regardless of difficulty, learning nothing all the while. In such circumstances the initial point of view becomes dictatorial. The Bible does not speak through the interpreter. Rather he manipulates the Bible so that it conforms to his presuppositions.

If all interpretation is carried on from within a particular context by an interpreter with a particular point of view, it is vain to ask for a final, definitive interpretation that rises above all individual approaches. It is impossible to imagine how such an interpretation could come into being, and, even supposing it could, it would necessarily be impersonal and static. All men belong to a specific time and place, and that is where the Bible must meet them. Through the particular interpreter, limited as he is, it does.

It follows that, when one reads works of interpretation, the provenance of the work must be borne in mind. In this field, more than in any other, the student needs to know something about the author. The simplest procedure for the beginner is to read books written from within his own context. If author and reader have the same presuppositions, some of the problems raised in this chapter will not arise. More experienced students will want to read books of wide renown regardless of their provenance, but they will be able to recognize the issues raised here and make allowances accordingly.

3

LANGUAGE, CULTURE AND MYTHOLOGY

In the last chapter we were primarily concerned with the interpreter himself. Now we return to the text. The author's meaning is enshrined in the text. Not perfectly, no doubt, because words on a page cannot do justice to the subtleties of communication between human subjects, but adequately. It is a written text, so the words lack the gestures, intonations and facial expressions which give life to conversation and which, no doubt, accompanied the biblical words when they were first uttered. It is a text in a foreign language, Hebrew with a little Aramaic for the Old Testament, Greek for the New Testament.

All languages have their subtleties. Every French boy and girl knows when to use *tu* and when to use *vous*. English has no equivalent distinction. What is the English translator to do when the word *tu* slips into the conversation in a French novel? Only in a roundabout way can he express the point that a relationship is moving into a new stage of intimacy.

All languages have refinements of this kind, not least the biblical languages, and many of them are not as easily defined as the difference between *tu* and *vous*. The Psalter constantly urges worshippers to wait upon God, but, had the Psalter been first written in English, the word 'wait' would rarely have been used. 'Waiting' covers so many conditions, from the expectant to the hopeless. The man in the condemned cell does not pass through the same experience as the mother-to-be, and neither has much in common with guerrilla fighters staging an ambush; but they are all waiting. In the Hebrew six different verbs are used and all refer to different aspects of the worshippers' attendance on God. The Psalter itself is not vague or confused, but confusion arises when different notions are rendered in English by the single word 'wait'.

Hebrew is a Semitic language. Its grammar, syntax and even

13

vocabulary bear little relation to those of English, or French, or Latin, or Greek. The interpreter therefore confronts a serious obstacle at the beginning of his task, as he needs to know exactly what the ancient text was saying. Fortunately commentaries exist which probe more deeply into the meaning of the text than any translation can do, but the undertaking is still considerable.

The Greek of the New Testament, *koinē* Greek, as it is called —which simply means common Greek—was the language of the market-place and more loosely constructed than the Greek of the great classical authors. As ancient languages go, New Testament Greek is not too difficult to learn, but it still throws up problems of vocabulary and syntax, partly, one suspects, because some New Testament contributors were more at home in Aramaic than in the Greek they were actually writing. Often problems lurk in the most unlikely places. 'Christ died for our sins', says Paul boldly, but what does that word 'for' mean? Prepositions are notoriously difficult to translate and Paul's *huper* is no exception. There may have been Greek-speakers in Corinth who were not entirely clear, for there is a certain breadth in the meaning of *huper*. Unfortunately that breadth does not correspond with the breadth of the word 'for', so simple translation provides no way out. The interpreter has to get back through the language right into the mind of Paul.

A kindred problem is that every language is deeply rooted in the culture in which it is used. Words are not clearly defined signals but rather pointers to particular experiences. Consequently many of them are properly understood only by those who share a common life with the writer. Such words can be known only from within, as it were. Can anyone who lives in the southern hemisphere fully comprehend what Christmas means in Europe? Experience of warm fires and good food set against the cold darkness outside gives the word 'Christmas' much of its sense. This can be explained, but it needs to be felt.

In the same way the seasons of the Bible are not easily understood. For the biblical writer nature dies in summer when the grass shrivels, flowers fade, and everywhere green gives way to grey. Rain in autumn brings promise of new life. This sense of the seasons gives rise to much biblical symbolism. Similarly

14

the word 'light', which to the ancient Hebrew meant a flickering wick at night or a blazing sun by day carries with it notions of both security and danger that are not understood in urban culture. A society with no taps but common experience of drought and a folk memory of devastating floods produced a symbolism of water that is not easily communicated to modern readers. And what of God who is addressed as Father? Fatherhood as a biological function may be the same everywhere but, socially, notions of fatherhood vary enormously. How can one know what the Bible means, unless one comprehends Hebrew social and family structure?

A further difficulty is that all cultures create or borrow, and then give currency to, particular cosmologies and mythologies that become the framework for literary expression. Questions of how the world came into being, where the gods live, what kind of life the dead lead are commonly answered in the form of myths. The word 'myth' gives rise to much misunderstanding, as it is often used negatively to mean a story that is not true. Myth, however, is a cultural necessity. When men attempt to discuss realities, unseen and intangible but none the less held to be realities, they have no alternative to talking about them in terms of the concrete, tangible world. In this way myths are born. Mythologies are many and various and, generally speaking, there is nothing sacrosanct about them. As tribes grow, change, and coalesce with others, mythologies become mixed.

It may appear that mythologies belong to anthropologists, but it is not so; for the Bible, like every ancient literature, is written in terms of one particular mythology. Man is made from the white ash of burnt-up Titans, according to the Greek myth of Zagreus, and from the blood of a rebellious god, according to one of the myths of Babylon. In Genesis man is made from the dust of the earth, God breathing into his nostrils the breath of life. Whatever we may think of other mythologies, the Genesis myth cannot be passed to the anthropologists, because Jewish and Christian doctrines of man stand firmly on that story.

The traditional comment of Jews and Christians has been that, though mythologies around the world might be interesting, they were purely imaginative; the biblical mythology reflected the true nature of things. In the Middle Ages that position was tenable; but once Copernicus and Galileo had shown that the earth revolved around the sun, grave problems arose. A clear example is in the ascension story in Acts 1. If the sky is a dome that covers the earth, and if God sits in the middle of it, so that he can see everything that happens below, the account of the ascension is comprehensible as both fact and metaphor. Jesus bade farewell to his friends on earth and was lifted up through the air till he joined his Father in the heavens. So Jesus is no longer physically apprehensible but he is universally present. No orthodox Christian of today would surrender the metaphorical truth of the ascension, but the mythology that holds the metaphor cannot now command respect. This paradox confronts the interpreter with one of his gravest problems. The biblical writers could not possibly have written in any other terms than their culture provided. We, for our part, cannot accept all those terms. So, even when the languages have been learnt and usages grasped, the matter of mythology still needs to be resolved.[1]

None of these difficulties carries the implication that the biblical text is deficient. As long as the earth remains, every account of the nature of God and his ways with men will have to be expressed through the medium of an imperfect language, with a finite vocabulary, and in terms of myth and metaphor that speak only obliquely of the matter in hand. It has often been argued that, given that limitations of this kind are inevitable, the Semitic background provides a language and culture well suited to the noble function required of it. Be that as it may, the interpreter has to expound the Bible so that the meaning intended by the first authors, writing from within their ancient and distant context, is conveyed to readers or hearers in his own decade. This is more than translation. It is 'transculturization', an ugly word for a complicated task.

A few simple illustrations will help to make this process clear. When Paul wrote 1 Cor. 13, he was fortunate to have at hand the Greek word *agapē* to represent the particular Christian disposition with which he was concerned. The fact that he used *agapē* made it plain that he was not talking about passion, nor about friendship, but about a new spiritual gift granted by divine grace

[1] This problem of mythologies receives a full treatment together with a radical solution in chapter 16.

16

to believers in Christ. How much of this was originally conveyed by the AV's 'charity' is hard to say, but what has happened to the word 'charity'? It has acquired overtones of self-righteousness and patronage. The new versions opt for 'love'. At points like this translation simply falls short. Careful exploration of the whole linguistic background alone suffices.

Another example of the need for interpretation is provided by Paul's words in 1 Cor. 11 requiring women to cover their heads in worship and men to wear their hair short. Paul is locked up securely within his own first-century Jewish culture. The task of the interpreter is to understand the social norms of the Corinthian streets as well as those of the primitive Church and to be familiar with Jewish beliefs about guardian angels; then he must build a bridge to our decade and say as precisely as he can how the spirit of Paul's utterance is to be applied today. So great is the interpreter's task. And these two illustrations belong to a relatively simple area!

Much discussion takes place nowadays about how one should interpret those stories in the Gospels where illness is attributed to possession by demons. Demons do not belong to the realm of concrete experience, but they provide an explanation for the illness which is a concrete experience. So demons are credited with 'real' existence. This is a classic example of mythology.

Today these New Testament stories are interpreted in various ways. Some scholars regard them as dramatic symbolism rather than historical narrative; some tend to speak of psychological disorders giving rise to physical symptoms but amenable to non-physical cure; others accept the demon theory and see Jesus as supreme exorcist. These are by no means the only possibilities. They are simply examples of different ways in which interpreters grapple with a piece of mythology. Further consideration of the miracle stories will be given in Chapter 5.

Even thornier problems arise when one considers concepts of time, of personality, of the being of God and, as we have seen, of the structure of the universe. Here, too, interpreters take widely different lines. Some stand aghast at the cultural chasm and consider that their task is to take the sense of the biblical passages and to represent it to this generation in an entirely new format. Others minimize the cultural gap and present biblical teaching as far as possible in biblical forms. Such divergences will be discussed again in Part 2 of this book. For the moment it is necessary only to notice the issues raised by the differences in language and culture between the biblical world and our own.

4

FACT AND RECORD

One of the clearest examples of cultural relativity lies in the different attitudes taken in different societies to the question of history. The deeper one probes into the Bible the clearer it becomes that it contains a notion of history considerably at odds with the one current in western culture.

Broadly speaking, history can be discussed in terms of three different elements. In the first place, there is the concrete event or series of events: the battle of Hastings, the Boston Tea Party, the signing of Magna Carta, the crossing of the Red Sea. These events were constituted by the actions of real people in relation to real physical factors. A real King John signed a real piece of parchment on a real island in the Thames. The event may have involved words, either spoken or written, but the fact that words can survive is, at this point, irrelevant. It is the act of signing that constitutes the event. Similarly, the battle of Hastings was constituted by men and horses and bows and arrows and the Exodus by fugitives and pursuers, water, wind and sand.

This element in history, real as it may have been, is irrecoverable now. Battle Abbey stands serenely on the spot where Harold died. We may see, in our mind's eye, hordes of Normans galloping over the hill, but they are no part of the real event. The battle is over and there is no point in cheering in the hope that Harold may yet win.

The second element is the evidence. How do we know that there was a battle of Hastings? Because words and pictures and less tangible things, like the Norman influence in our culture, survive into the present. The event and the evidence are separate things. A criminal trial rests on the fact that an irrecoverable event has taken place. If that event could be reconstituted, there would be no need for a trial, but it is of the nature of events that it cannot be. So evidence is produced. Some of it will be words spoken by witnesses recounting impressions that are lodged in the memory. Some of it will be concrete objects— clothing, weapons, fingerprints, etc. These alone can lead to a verdict. Without them the criminal would always escape, his evil deeds hidden irretrievably in the past.

The third element in history is judgement. The historian has to examine the evidence, assess it, and then construct his own account of what happened; and, even beyond that, he has to put forward theories of the relation of events in a series to one another. Very little evidence is unambiguous. Witnesses suffer limitations: they see the event from one point of view only, their memories are imperfect, they are often unable to describe adequately what they have seen, they are amenable to suggestion. Consequently the historian is never in a position to *know* exactly what happened. Even supposing he were, he would still want to say why it happened and how this particular event related to others in a series. He brings to the study of history, therefore, both personal skills and personal judgement.

This is history more or less as we understand it. It is now necessary to ask whether the biblical writers held a similar view. Unfortunately they lacked our resources for reconstructing the past. The modern historian makes use of libraries, archives, museums, contemporary records and artefacts, archaeological discoveries, highly technical means of dating objects, and so on. The biblical writer, lacking these resources, found himself very short of evidence, but seems not to have been concerned. He carried on writing history without raising problems of evidence. This is explained partly by his reliance on oral tradition, which, though quite different from evidence, may take the place of evidence in a particular kind of scheme, and partly by his lack of interest in the views and reactions of disinterested observers. One gains the impression that, if the records of the Egyptian War Office had been available to the authors of Exod. 14, they would not have bothered to consult them.

Why is this so? Why, from beginning to end, do the biblical authors, who are profoundly interested in the events of the past, fail to prove any of their assertions by reference to the testimony of disinterested observers? In the case of the resurrection, it has been asked over and over again: why did not Jesus appear to known sceptics to prove his triumph incontrovertibly? Why do the Gospels confine themselves to what one must call prejudiced witness? The answer is that the biblical historian does not make the distinction that we consistently make between the hard facts of the event and the thoughts of the one who reflects upon them. His only concern is with facts grasped in a certain way. The happening and the grasping are both essential to the event. Anyone who looks on and fails to grasp in that particular way is a false witness. The true event has escaped him.

This understanding of the complementary nature of events and observers makes sense when it is set within the Hebrew account of reality. To the Hebrew, the first fact in every situation is God. Only those happenings in which the divine ordering is manifest are true and memorable. The others, and obviously there must have been others, are hollow and insignificant. They are best forgotten as non-events, and this reckoning holds good no matter how important these happenings may be in terms of secular history. Fortunately there are other happenings in which the divine purpose is not only formative but apparent, at least to inspired observers. These are true events. They witness to the true nature of things because God is seen to be the originator of them, he displays his purpose through them, and that purpose is grasped by faithful observers. The true event, therefore, has a composite structure, namely: the purpose of God—the happening—subsequent apprehension of the purpose through the happening. To observe the middle term without being aware of the other two, as the stranger or the unbeliever does, is to mark the external form and miss the true event altogether.

This explains why the biblical historian is content with oral tradition. For him it is the third term that matters, the apprehension of the divine purpose. The oral tradition begins with those who apprehend that purpose in some particular happening and is continued exclusively by those who share the apprehension. As the tradition passes from believer to believer, the apprehension is strengthened, so that, curiously, the historian of the sixth century B.C. has a firmer grasp of the event of the Exodus than a person, even a Hebrew, who was on the spot. Consequently objections against reliance on oral tradition often miss the point. If hard facts are being sought, oral tradition, for all its tendency to become fixed and stable, is of little use, but, if the end is

21

faithful apprehension of the divine purpose, oral tradition is admirably suited to achieving it.

Further inquiry into what the Bible means by divine purpose makes this point even more emphatic. In the Bible revelation is never static. God does not reveal himself in order to tidy up theological conceptions. He reveals himself as power in action. Events are, thus, centres of power. The biblical writer and the ordinary Hebrew took it for granted that rehearsing the record of these dynamic events would liberate the saving power afresh, that is, allow it to continue its creative course through history. This is exactly what the Hebrew cult attempted to do. Remembering the past was not simply a stirring of the emotions, still less a mental exercise; it was rather a formal re-living of the great event. How it was done is difficult to say. Recital played a part and drama too, but Hebrew theology also came into it. Through the original event God acted on Israel's behalf and Israel knew it. God does not change his nature nor cease his activity. What he did once he will do again.

It must have been obvious to every Hebrew worshipper, as it is obvious to every Jew who celebrates the Passover today, that the actual physical conditions of the escape from Egypt can never be reconstructed; but this does not matter because the other two terms of the event, the divine purpose and its apprehension, can be repeated. Words or drama can replace the middle term, the happening, so the whole event is virtually repeatable. Through cultic celebration the event of Exodus takes place year after year, and year after year Israel experiences God's saving power. This is how history is understood in the Bible.

This view of history is a far cry from the one with which this chapter began. Event-evidence-interpretation give one pattern. Divine purpose-happening-apprehension and record-cultic repetition give an entirely different pattern. History written in terms of the latter scheme cannot simply be read off by a reader schooled in the former as if it belonged to his own world.

Each interpreter finds his own way. There are some who, while perfectly aware of the arguments of this chapter, still regard the actual happening as of supreme importance, because for them the happening created the faith. It then follows that, if faith is to continue, the happening must be proved over and over again. Those who approach the matter in this way must beware

22

of arguing in a circle. If the happening itself is crucial, evidence must be available to prove it. The evidence for the biblical happenings comes almost exclusively from the Bible itself. Now in no way can it be argued that the Bible, as it stands, proves to the satisfaction of the sceptic the factual nature of the happenings recorded in it. The Bible 'proves' this kind of truth only to those who already have a robust faith. So the circle is closed. Faith is necessary to believe in the happenings that give rise to faith. One must, therefore, approach with caution the kind of book that treats biblical history as accurate in the way that we understand historical accuracy.

At the other extreme are interpreters who hold that hard facts have no relevance to faith or to biblical interpretation. For them the Bible is a book of faith rather than fact, and the true historical encounter is not between God and Moses on a distant mountain, but between God and the hearer when the Bible is read and its message preached. Interpreters of this kind can be very sceptical of the factual nature of incidents recorded in the Bible. The danger here is that the whole area of historical fact is surrendered. There are no inescapable facts that stand sentinel over the argument. History is something private to the individual. Faith speaks to faith. The unbelieving observer is left outside the game.

Between these two ways of handling the issue of history in the Bible there are many others; we shall encounter them later. One thing is certain: no method of interpretation has any claim to our support if it does not treat this topic with the utmost seriousness.

5

MIRACLE

To some extent the question of miracle raises matters of fact and evidence, to some extent it hinges on cultural attitudes to the natural order and the possibility of divine intervention within it. In either case the topic follows naturally on the discussion of the last two chapters. So intricate are the issues raised, so varied and numerous the treatments of them, that it is necessary to spell out clearly what is being attempted here. We are concerned with the biblical conception of the miraculous, with the definition, elucidation and analysis of the miracle stories. The aim is to understand the problems that miracle stories present to the interpreter. The question whether miracles, by any definition, are possible or impossible, and the further question whether any particular miracle actually took place are, as far as possible, avoided.

The word 'miracle' comes from a Latin verb meaning 'to wonder'. A miracle is an event that causes people to wonder. That raises a question straightaway. Which people? The phenomena that are regarded as wonderful vary from society to society. To some extent the readiness of a people to accept the miraculous into their thought world is in inverse ratio to their familiarity with empirical science. The simple society finds so many mysterious things in the creation, so many things to wonder at, that it will accept the category of miracle without hesitation. Perhaps it would be truer to say that their world of phenomena is not properly differentiated—not properly, that is to say, by our standards. More sophisticated societies tend to be more sceptical. Consequently, even when causes of wonder arise, the wonder tends to be in a lower key. We may be mystified by snake charmers, people who walk barefoot on red-hot cinders, practitioners of acupuncture, and so on, but we would not call them miracle-workers. We work on the principle that there must be an explanation somewhere.

Ancient Israel had little knowledge of empirical science. Perhaps, from time to time, there were experiments and discoveries relating to medicine or irrigation or breeding cattle or making war, but the Bible tells us nothing about them. Discovery, in that sense, appears not to have stimulated Hebrew imagination. The world of the unseen and the inexplicable were understood in terms of mythology. A non-empirical universe was constructed in order to make sense out of things. Here the Hebrew imagination came into play. Angels and messengers appear to do their Lord's bidding, God himself intervenes with a mighty hand and an outstretched arm, demons afflict the unrighteous, the natural order breaks its own bounds, the seas pile up and the shadow goes backwards. Those who gave us the Bible were not greatly interested in the regular, ordered universe with which science is concerned, and they do not hesitate to express in miraculous terms events that we should explain naturally.

This observation does not solve the problem of miracles, but it does provide a pointer. Hebrew society accepted the idea of the miraculous readily. If it does not sound too paradoxical, it treated the miraculous as normal. In a mysterious world mysterious happenings were to be expected.

The most interesting fact about Israel's mythology was not that it was unscientific but that it was informed by a vigorous theology. The mystery of events was a divine mystery. God was the great Cause. By this reckoning, a miracle was a practical event that required for its explanation the intrusion into the normal course of things of the divine power. The sun stood still at Beth-horon, fire fell from heaven on Carmel, the storm was stilled at Gennesaret, the tomb was empty, because God was at work to save his own. Even in those cases where it would seem only reasonable to consider secondary causes—at Beth-horon the ambushed Amorites had the slope, the hail and a seasoned army to contend with—the Bible does not waver. The divine factor outweighs all other factors. That is the message again and again.

For this reason little time will be given here to the supposition that the biblical miracles were simply exaggerations of natural

25

events. To explain the Exodus as a natural, fortuitous happening that has been magnified out of all proportion by Jewish tradition is to part company completely with the Bible. It may be that some stories were exaggerated or, at least, made more emphatic in transmission. It may be that some of them do in fact relate to natural events. But this explanation diverts attention from the significant point that in the wonderful event God was revealing his hand.

In these circumstances one would expect the content of the miracle stories to reflect the awesome theological background and, with few exceptions, that is what we find. In some mythologies sportive deities cavort with goddesses, godlike heroes slay dragons, warriors are protected by magic. But who could confuse that kind of mythology with what we find in the Bible? There is a sobriety, a deep, searching seriousness about even the most improbable biblical stories. Not all of them are on the same level. Here and there, as for example in the Elisha cycle (2 Kings 2—13), the text records miracles that satisfy ephemeral needs. But such accounts are so exceptional that the gravity of the common biblical miracle is underlined.

Miracle stories in all cultures are, in one sense, symbolic. They are vivid, dramatic expressions of the true nature of things. The miracles that attend Perseus and Hercules demonstrate that, mysterious and unpredictable as the universe is, it favours the chosen few, the dashing heroes, the brilliant lovers. The biblical stories equally convey their message. Miracles belong to the Holy God and therefore to Israel his chosen, to his servants like Elijah, and supremely to Jesus. The right way to read the stories is to see them as displays in particular situations of what God intends universally. When the healing of the paralytic in Mark 2.1–12 was recounted in the days of the primitive Church, the comment would not have been, 'How lucky that particular peasant was!' Rather those early Christians would have asked, 'What is our paralysis, and how are we healed?' The interpreter still asks the same questions.

The first question the interpreter has to settle, therefore, is whether he is dealing with a series of miraculous happenings or with stories which may or may not have some basis in fact but which are primarily significant *as stories*.

The former alternative carries us out of the realm of biblical

26

interpretation. We can comment on how the Bible records events, on editorial practices and the presuppositions of particular authors, but the real issue is the fact of the miracle, and this goes beyond biblical study into the realm of philosophy of religion. That is not our field. Here we simply concentrate on the biblical records and see what is involved in the assumption that they are, broadly speaking, factual.

One question that arises with every story is: what precisely is being asserted as having happened? To say 'The man was healed' is vague. Leprosy and paralysis result in physical changes to the body. In one case, cells die and disappear, in the other, muscles suffer wastage. One wants to know whether cells were instantly created to restore limbs to their proper shape, and whether muscles were instantly reconstituted. Similar questions have to be asked about chemical changes in the brain, normally regarded as irreversible, that follow closely on death.

The sensitive nature of this kind of question is best revealed by taking an extreme example. In the story of the nativity, the star 'came and stood over where the young child was' (Matt. 2.9). As long as one believes stars to be lantern-like objects secured in place in a not-too-distant sky, the possibility of one star descending to point out a path and finally to indicate a particular stable is conceivable. With our understanding of stars, we know that the most the wise men could have gained is a single compass bearing, a dubious aid since they knew where they were going and found their way to Bethlehem by other means. So the question arises again: what is being asserted as having happened?

At this point the interpreter has to make a decision. He must either decide that the facts of the case cannot be altogether as the Bible states, or he must assert that God can do anything, and so seek a solution that is uncompromisingly supernatural. The first alternative means that interest is transferred from the facts to the story, a position that we shall discuss later. The second raises the further question of evidence. If the critical factor is what precisely took place as a result of God's intervention, then one must ask: what kind of evidence is necessary to convince a reasonable person that it was indeed so?

The extreme improbability of some of the events recorded makes this question of evidence critical. The murder of Mariamne

27

by Herod is accepted by the average reader on the basis of Josephus' account because it accords with everything that is known of Herod, but the spontaneous creation or destruction of body cells is not so readily accepted.[1] To take a modern example, no one doubts that there was a Christmas truce on the western front in 1914, but who believes that angels appeared at Mons to guide the troops in retreat? The latter event does not lack testimony, but it is not taken seriously by historians. What kind of evidence would be necessary to convince them that there were angels at Mons? Evidently the testimony of a few embattled soldiers is not enough.

From a historical point of view, the evidence for the biblical miracles is slight. The biblical text alone provides it. It is possible to argue from the contention that God can do anything to the conclusion that the Bible possesses unique authority as a witness, but this is an argument of faith. There is no logical reason to suppose that the Bible cannot err, and those who make the supposition do so on grounds other than logic. Here again one must beware of arguing in a circle. How does one know that the Bible is true? By faith. On what is faith based? On the Bible.

On these terms, those who do not believe and who consequently find the evidence for the miracles inadequate will never be able to understand what the Bible is saying. Some interpreters do not flinch from this conclusion. 'The natural man receiveth not the things of the Spirit of God: for they are foolishness unto him; and he cannot know them, because they are spiritually judged' (1 Cor. 2.14). On these premises, there is little point in arguing about miracles and the biblical records. One simply prays that the eyes of the blind will be opened.

There are others, however, who find it impossible to accept the argument of the last page or two and who are concerned to express the reasonable nature of the Word of God. Such interpreters are impelled towards the conclusion that the biblical miracles must be studied primarily as stories rather than as facts. To this view we now turn.

To the author of today it matters that he should get his facts

[1] See Flavius Josephus, *Antiquities of the Jews*, 15.7.5. Josephus was a Jewish historian who fought against the Romans in the rebellion of A.D. 66. Thereafter he went to Rome where he wrote his voluminous and invaluable history of the Jews.

28

straight, and he can go to libraries and consult newspapers and archives and the other treasuries of a literate society. The biblical author, whether concerned about positive facts or not, had nowhere to go. He had to rely on oral tradition. If at any point along the way the story he received had been moulded to make it convey its message more clearly, the final editor would have had no means of knowing it. Historical accuracy in our sense was beyond him.

Whether this mattered or not depends upon the purpose for which the story was preserved. If it was to supply positive history, then the lack of resources was a disaster. But was it? Did the biblical author set out to write positive history and fail, or did he set out to write some other kind of narrative and succeed? Let us assume the latter. What exactly was the writer doing?

When Christianity burst into the Graeco-Roman world, Christian affirmation became technical and philosophical, but it was not so in the Hebrew milieu where the first elements of the gospel were formed. The Hebrew linguistic style was ideally suited to narrative. The Hebrew culture—and both testaments belong to Hebrew culture—was not given to discussing the ways of God or the divinity of Christ in the abstract. A Greek might compose a subtle treatise on such subjects, but a Hebrew would be likely to tell a story, like the parable of the labourers in the vineyard (Mark 12.1–12).

It is to be expected, then, that the majesty of God will be expressed in stories that show him riding high over the creation, creating and re-creating at will. Deep and ultimate convictions about the nature of Jesus will be asserted in stories of his doing the things that only God can do, stilling the storm, raising the dead, bringing divine order out of demon-ridden chaos. How the matter of the story relates to the historical facts of the case may now be impossible to determine. It does not follow that, because the story has a theological purpose, it is necessarily non-factual, but the factual element is not primary.

The miraculous element is, on this reckoning, no embarrassment at all. Not even the star over the stable or the sun standing still in the heavens creates problems. The biblical writer knew what he wanted to say. His statements made sense in the world as he understood it. What we have to do is to grasp the theological affirmations of the stories while setting the physical details on one side. The miraculous element can then be accepted boldly, for non-miraculous stories would not make the point.

The issue of miracles has tended to polarize discussion of the Bible, particularly of the New Testament. Some have insisted on their factual nature and been loath to allow any other interpretation. Others have been impressed by the theological and christological import of the New Testament incidents and have lost interest in the factual element. There is no need for such complete polarity. Indeed, there can hardly be any doubt that, while not all the stories are true, they are not all literary constructions either. Judicious interpretation demands an assessment of both theological purpose and historical probability. Here, more than anywhere, the interpreter has to wait and listen to hear what the Bible is really saying.

6

THE UNITY OF THE BIBLE

Many people take the unity of the Bible for granted. Superficially there are good reasons for doing so. The Bible comes to us as a book with many parts, but all are bound in a single volume. It is on view in places of worship, and public readings are drawn from every part. One hears preachers using the phrase 'The Bible says ...' as if, on any given subject, the biblical point of view could be established without difficulty. Furthermore, there is a certain logic in the argument that if, as is presumed by Jews and Christians alike, the Bible, defined as they define it, has a relevance to this day and every day, it must have a coherent and discernible message. So there emerges a conception of 'the Bible' as a unitary phenomenon in the world of religion.

There are those who regard the unity of the Bible as a function of its sanctity and, consequently, are unwilling to subject it to critical scrutiny. Many more suffer a shock when they discover how far-reaching the effects of critical scrutiny can be. The integrity of the Word of God seems to them to fade away, leaving behind only the miscellaneous literature of a distant people, interesting and instructive no doubt, but lacking the mystique of 'the Bible'.

In fact it is unjust to blame the critics. Thorny questions soon present themselves to every reader of the Bible. There are the differences between the testaments, the brutal passages that fit in so ill with much of the rest of biblical teaching, the contradictions, small but sometimes significant, that appear whenever two or more passages treat the same subject. How does one solve these problems?

At this point the interpreter has to decide whether to go on or to go back. If he pursues these questions, others will arise, and he will find himself working through the whole critical programme. If the questions are resisted, an uneasy peace can

31

be maintained. The unity and sanctity of the Bible will remain, unquestioned and unquestionable, but will conversation with the rest of the world be possible? The point of view adopted in this chapter is that the question must be pursued. That does not mean that the notion of unity is surrendered. The simplistic notion of the single, holy volume will disappear and the great diversity of the literature within will come to light; but the question of unity will be raised again, so that it can be established, if it is established, on a more secure foundation.

The Bible contains many different types of literature—myths, sagas, legends, hymns, records, laws, letters, oracles, etc. The subject matter varies enormously. Some books look forward, some look back; some plot the ways of God, others meditate on the human condition; some are full of poetic vision, others of mundane, not to say prudential, advice. The age of the biblical material also varies. No one can say when the earliest words of the Old Testament were spoken, nor even when they were written down, but most would agree that some compositions from David's reign in the tenth century B.C. have survived. That means that, in terms of written documents, the first is separated from the last by some eight centuries. Another two hundred and fifty years must be added to embrace the New Testament. As a written composition, then, the Bible is the work of at least a thousand years.

None of these facts weighs very heavily against unity. It is possible for a myth, a hymn and a letter, however different in style, to present the same view of life and for books on different subjects and of different ages to contribute to the same theology. It is not easy to distil a single biblical notion from an apocalyptic vision, a piece of sage counsel, and a story from the Gospels, but it is not antecedently impossible.

More serious difficulties arise when it becomes clear that different books have different aims, record different facts, presume different world views, and expound different notions of God. The divergence between Old and New Testaments will be treated in a separate chapter, but there are many other examples.

Scholars of a few decades ago made much of the divergence between prophetic and priestly religion. Prophets, it was said, served God by justice and mercy, priests by spotless sacrifice.

Many prophetic passages, like Isa. 1.10–17 and Amos 5.21–5, poured scorn on priestly notions of righteousness. No doubt too much was made of this; contemporary differences between preachers and ritualists were being read back into the Old Testament; but even so, the distinction between the two conceptions of divine service cannot be completely resolved. Prophecy lived by protest, priesthood by ritual exercise. As long as both remained, there was a continuing tension between Israel's formal cult and the prophetic vision. Whatever unity arose grew out of paradox.

Prophets are also to be distinguished from the apocalyptists who succeeded them. Both looked to the future and both were concerned with the salvation of Israel after judgement had been fairly dispensed. But, whereas the prophets could see the pattern working itself out in terms of this world's history, the apocalyptists abandoned hope for this world. They saw only a total destruction of this dispensation and the creation of a new one. Here is a difference of world view. Is this world ultimately to be redeemed or to be destroyed? It is a very topical question. The Bible does not give a consistent answer.

The Bible is concerned with history, but the historical theme does not provide a unifying factor. At the heart of biblical history is the belief that God intervenes in the affairs of men, against all regularity, to bring about his will. There is, however, a less well-known strand in the Bible, the Wisdom literature, in which the ways of God are plotted in terms of unchanging moral realities. It is hard to equate the God of Exod. 14 with the God of Prov. 14.

The history books themselves see things from different angles. The Deuteronomic History, that great work which runs through Joshua, Judges, 1 and 2 Samuel and 1 and 2 Kings, differs from the Priestly History found in 1 and 2 Chronicles, Ezra and Nehemiah. Both recount facts to magnify their own interests. The Deuteronomic History was written to show how the divine pattern, set out in Judg. 3.7–11, had worked itself out in Israel's history. The Priestly History stressed and glorified all things priestly; Levites, for example, sparsely mentioned in Samuel and Kings, appear in Chronicles at every turn of the road. The two histories often give different accounts of the same incident. In the story of the bringing of the Ark from the house of Obed-edom

33

up to the city of David, 2 Sam. 6 describes a modest procession, a violent, uncontrolled dance by David, and a consequent altercation between David and his wife, Michal. 1 Chron. 15 records an endless procession of officials accompanied by full orchestra; the dance, its objectionable nature, and Michal's displeasure are squeezed into half a verse. John and the Synoptic Gospels, and Acts and the writings of Paul can be compared in the same way. The question is whether the two points of view can reasonably be synthesized.

It is necessary to consider what is meant by unity. Unity is not so much a quality of the facts themselves as a function of the mind of the observer. If there is a basket containing a dozen apples and a dozen oranges, it may appear that the apples are a unity and that so too are the oranges. But if two shoppers, unloading the basket, apply the concept of 'mine and yours', six apples and six oranges will make a unity, and the unity of oranges as oranges will be irrelevant.

From a literary point of view, the first five books are by no means a unity. Different material from different periods has been worked over by different hands, but it was seen to be one in the sense that it all bore witness to Israel's troubled, but divinely ordained, path through history. So the Torah came into being. The *disparate* nature of the material is as clear now as ever it was, but the *unity* of the Torah has been lived out by devout Jews of so many generations that now it would be absurd to deny it. These books both are and are not a unity. It all depends on the criteria which are being used in the assessment.

It is now possible to consider ways in which the Bible, for all the diversity discussed above, might be regarded as a unity. If there is any such unity, it will be complex, for no argument that all the books have the same unmistakable message will convince. None the less if unity cannot be established in some way, it is hard to see how interpretation can survive. One can interpret all the works of a particular author or all the books of a decade on, shall we say, euthanasia, but not fifty books picked at random from the shelves of different libraries. If there is no unity at all, there is no interpretation.

Success with regard to the Bible will depend on the interpreter's willingness to accept a relative unity. If every word has to be brought into line, the cause is lost. If, however, selection and rejection of material are allowable, if some sectors can be given prominence at the expense of others, the task can proceed.

The approaches of interpreters vary. Let us consider three representative lines of argument.

First, it is possible to pitch the debate on a relatively low theological level and to contend for a unity that is simply cultural. The Bible is the product of a people who lived for two thousand years at the western end of the fertile crescent and who experienced a constant climate and, broadly speaking, the same physical conditions of life. The language developed, but it was a continuous development. The change from Hebrew to Aramaic in the second century B.C. did not destroy the continuity, and even the adoption of Greek did not involve as profound a change as may appear, for much of the New Testament is Greek in a Hebraic style. The economy, the social structure, the customs and conventions, the administration of justice, the religious rites, the cosmology, the mythology, all these reveal not constancy but continuity. It is true that there was no political continuity, that there were deportations and invasions, that the great empires, Persian, Greek and Roman, had a profound influence on Hebrew culture. But it is still reasonable to see the Bible as the product of a single, developing group. Unity of this kind is relative but undeniable. The question is whether it is significant. It is not easy to see how the homogeneity of the Bible in cultural terms is helpful to those who are interpreting the Bible today.

Second, it is possible to argue that the unity of the Bible rests on its continuing concern with the same religious ideas. The holiness of God, his control of history, his covenant with his chosen people, the quest for righteousness, the need for sacrifice, these recur again and again. One might say that the Bible records a thousand years' reflection on these religious themes. When Paul argues in Romans about the justice of God in his ways with men, he is heir to the understanding of the prophets, lawyers, priests and holy men of Israel's history. If the reader believes that these themes relate directly to man's eternal salvation, he will see here a coherent development of much significance. It is not established beyond all possible dispute. Relevant material has to be stressed and irrelevant has to be ignored. The contention that these themes are eternally significant is a judgement of value. Nevertheless, if these moves are accepted, there is

35

here a reasonable way of affirming the unity of the Bible.

Third, it is possible to be dogmatic and affirm that the unity of the Bible rests on God's continuous purpose. This is to turn the argument round. The other approaches begin with the Bible to see if unity can be found in it. This approach begins with a prior conviction and lays the onus on the interpreter to uncover the unity that must be there. The difficulty is that the premise is so substantial. Empirical arguments are waved aside. One works by faith alone. For some this will be the supreme merit of the approach; for others it will be an impossible stumbling-block.

There are many other ways of looking at the problem. None finds perfect consistency in the Bible; all have different conceptions of what the unity is. This hard but crucial fact reveals both the significance and the delicacy of the issue.

7

THE RELATION OF OLD TESTAMENT
TO NEW TESTAMENT

The question of the relation between the Old and New Testaments
is a specifically Christian problem. Judaism venerates the Torah,
the Prophets and the Writings as Holy Scripture and is not
concerned with what Christians call the New Testament. For
Judaism, the Old Testament is not old but ever new; the so-
called New Testament is an error and a deviation; there was
no dislocation of Israel's religion in the first Christian century
and no new revelation surpassing the Torah.

For Christians it is otherwise. Christians label the Jewish Scriptures 'old' deliberately. They mean that there was an old
dispensation that reached an end and a new one that replaced
it; and the term 'Holy Scripture' embraces both. This raises
questions about the authority and value of the old and about the
relation of the old to the new. The rich history of Judaism rules
out simplistic resolutions of this issue. If the history of Israel
were an uncomplicated account of progress towards the birth
of Jesus, if the Old Testament proclaimed itself to be transient
and limited, this chapter would present no problem. But Judaism,
by its vitality and permanence, forbids such hypotheses. Jews
and Christians both look back to the same historical sources.
Wherein lies the true continuity?

This is the oldest of all problems for Christian interpreters,
and it is instructive to see how the earliest Christians tried
to resolve it. They did not find the solution easy. They believed
that God had called Israel, that he had made promises to her,
raised up inspired men in her midst, revealed to her again and
again his holy will. They believed, as most first-century Jews
believed, that nothing could prevent the fulfilment of the
promises, but—this was the great divide—Christians asserted

37

that the climax of history *had* arrived, that the Messiah *had* appeared, that the first act of the drama in which all promises would be fulfilled *had* already been played out. Jews asserted that it was not so.

This was an appalling problem for those who proclaimed that Jesus was the Christ. If they were right, it meant that the nation that for two millennia had been nurtured by God as his own chosen people had failed to recognize his greatest gift when it came. Moreover, certain Gentiles, who were no part of the chosen people, seemed to recognize what Israel failed to recognize and to demonstrate all the signs of having been received, forgiven and empowered by God. Could it be that the divine plan had miscarried, that two thousand years of preparation had proved both ineffectual and unnecessary?

This problem agitated the earliest Christians more than any other. Different answers were put forward and deep dissension afflicted the Church. Paul has set down his ideas in Rom. 9—11, and his tortured logic shows how concerned he was to gather the disparate facts together into a coherent plan. Fundamentally Paul's problem is identical with that of the modern Christian interpreter. How does the history of Israel fit in with the history of early Christianity? How can the old and the new stand side by side as Holy Scripture?

The essential difference between old and new is that, whereas the Old Testament is concerned with Israel as a nation and God's dealings with her, the New Testament is concerned with one particular Israelite and the story of the sect that proclaimed him Lord. The first question then is: does the Old Testament look forward to such a climax, or is the change properly described as a dislocation, a break in continuity rather than a fulfilment?

This question directs attention towards the Messianic prophecies of the Old Testament. Christian apologists from earliest times have used these passages, which speak of a coming deliverer, as evidence that Jesus was in fact the divine fulfilment of Old Testament promises. When the nine lessons are read in King's College Chapel, Cambridge, every Christmas, the homogeneity of the Bible seems assured. Careful scrutiny of the Messianic passages and of Christian interpretation of them, however, leads to more restrained conclusions. It is by no

38

means evident that the Old Testament looks forward to one exactly like Jesus and to no other, nor that everything that Jesus said and did fulfils Old Testament expectation.

On one hand, an honest reading of the Old Testament material reveals a dazzling variety in what was expected, and no clear picture of a single Messiah. On the other hand, what we know of Jesus does not enable us to make precise correlations, between many of his actions and particular prophecies, and this despite the fact that New Testament writers have a tendency to strengthen the link whenever it is possible to do so.

A single example must suffice. The best known of all messianic prophecies is Isa. 7.14, quoted by Matthew (1.23) when recounting Joseph's vision before the birth of Jesus. 'Behold, a virgin shall conceive, and bear a son ...' All too readily Christians have said that here, seven centuries before the birth of Jesus, Isaiah was making a precise prediction of the event. But in the first place, Isaiah was speaking of his immediate situation, and the child belonged to it, for he was the sign of the remedy; secondly, the words quoted contain the only elements in the whole chapter that fit the story of the birth of Jesus; and thirdly, on Isaiah's lips, the prophecy was not messianic in the accepted Christian sense. He was speaking of a contemporary prince, not of an ultimate deliverer. Similar comments could be made about all the messianic passages of the Old Testament.

Isa. 7.14 is commonly regarded as the best example of messianic prophecy largely because of the appearance of the word 'virgin' in the English text. Much has been written on this. Suffice it to say that the Hebrew word does not mean 'virgin', that in Jewish tradition there was no expectation of a virgin-born Messiah, that the idea of virginity comes from the Greek text which appeared centuries after Isaiah was dead. This is not an argument for the *discontinuity* of Old Testament and New Testament. Isa. 7, like many other passages in the Old Testament, speaks of hope in affliction, divine deliverance when the enemy is at the gates. That itself is prophecy—not precise prophecy of Jesus, but general prophecy of the way in which God intervenes and gives signs of his coming. All the messianic passages testify to an intervening God and suggest much about the nature and quality of his intervention. Can it not be claimed that Jesus was the great intervention that brought all expectations into focus? Many Christian interpreters would argue in that way. The thesis is not as dramatic as the common one, but it stands much closer scrutiny.

The binding of Christian Bibles suggests that the New Testament is the proper conclusion of the Jewish literary tradition with the Apocrypha perhaps providing a bridge. That is not the whole truth. Jewish men of letters were anything but quiescent in the years after 164 B.C., which most people regard as the date of Daniel, the last book of the Old Testament to be written. Some of their writings are preserved in the Apocrypha but by no means all. A collection of the remainder was made in 1913 and published in English with the Apocrypha under the title *The Apocrypha and Pseudepigrapha of the Old Testament*.[1] There are also the scrolls from the Dead Sea. First-century Judaism was highly literate, and it is not obvious to an impartial observer that the writings of the New Testament provide the proper continuation of Jewish literary tradition. The word 'proper' highlights the problem. By what criterion does one determine that a particular event is the proper fulfilment of a prophecy or a particular book the proper continuation of a literary tradition?

The relation of the life and worship of the early Church to the Hebrew religious tradition is similarly contentious. There is a historical connection; but so there is between the Old Testament and Judaism. In Christianity the faith of Israel is broadened to include Gentiles; the blood sacrifice of the Temple is replaced by the sacrifice on Calvary; admission to the redeemed community is by faith and baptism, not birth and circumcision; believing the gospel takes the place of observing the Torah; the Eucharist overshadows all Jewish festivals. Is this fulfilment or deviation? There is no obvious empirical answer. The matter in the last resort is settled by faith. For Jews the New Testament is the product of an aberrant messianic sect; for Christians it is the divine fulfilment of the former covenant; for agnostics it is the random product of Jewish experience and hopes. The rest of this chapter will discuss various ways in which Christians have attempted to establish positive links between Old Testament and New Testament on a sure foundation.

[1] The editor was R. H. Charles.

Broadly speaking one can distinguish two kinds of approach. Some writers regard the New Testament as the cardinal revelation and consider the Old Testament only in the light of this fact. Others see the sacred history of Israel as a sustained revelation culminating in the supreme event of the incarnation.

Some in the first group argue that the revelation in Jesus acts as a judgement on the Old Testament. Paul's arguments in Galatians and Romans and Luther's reflections on them have given rise to a scholarly tradition that stresses the discontinuity between the testaments. By this reckoning the Old Testament is not Christian revelation at all. It does not even express the promise of better things to come, save the sense that the failure of one quest directs attention towards its opposite.

Still beginning with the New Testament, it is possible to understand the Old Testament in exactly the opposite way. If Jesus was 'the image of the invisible God, the first-born of all creation', if all things were created in him (Col. 1.15f.), there is, strictly speaking, no pre-Christian dispensation. God in Christ was revealing himself in Israel's history and waiting only for the final revelation in human flesh. Pursuing this line, scholars have produced Christian studies in which the Old Testament, even against its more obvious sense, is made into Christian Scripture. The integrity of the Old Testament in its own right seems not to be respected, but by this method a strong link between the testaments can be forged and a coherent account of biblical teaching can be constructed.

Taking the two testaments together one can proceed by recognizing within them a constant pattern of promise and fulfilment. Many times in the early stories of the Bible promises are made to Abraham: a great name, a great blessedness, a son, a land, a great posterity—all these will be his, and through his children all nations of the earth will be blessed (Gen. 12.3f.; 17.5f.; 18.18; 22.16ff.). As these promises are fulfilled other promises appear. 2 Sam. 7 recapitulates the promises made to Abraham and gives them a greater dimension. So, throughout the Old Testament, promises are made and fulfilled and renewed and fulfilled again. In the New Testament, too, fulfilment leads to promise and promise to fulfilment. If this is true on a small scale, may it not be true of the whole course of history? Is not the story of Israel one vast promise and the story of the New Testament a com-

41

plete fulfilment? If so, Old and New Testaments are bound together inextricably, each meaningless without the other; and the significance of the Bible is seen only in the Bible as a whole.

A similar approach concerns itself with what is known as typology. This is the theory that in Old Testament history we encounter persons, institutions and events which are divinely established models of corresponding realities in the New Testament. The correspondence is only in one or two features and, as in the case of Adam and Christ, may involve contrast as well as comparison; but the significance is clear. The Old Testament type is only a partial revelation, the first rays, as it were, of the New Testament dawn, but there is an essential consistency between the two. Typology differs from the theme of promise and fulfilment in that the type is concrete and objective and maybe not recognized until the anti-type has appeared, whereas the promise is verbal and necessarily leads to expectation. None the less the two methods go hand in hand, both seeing the saga of redemption as a continuing process in which the Old Testament has a clearly defined place.

In this area tidy categories are hard to establish. Most Christian interpreters are concerned to hold together the decisive significance of God's act in Christ and the historical background and preparation in Israel. Old and new must both be preserved without loss to either. This is a formidable task, but one no interpreter can avoid.

8

INSPIRATION

The preceding chapters point inevitably to the present one. If the Bible is so significant in the life of synagogue and church, and if it is held in some way or another to be unique, then the question of inspiration cannot be shirked. Can the Bible be satisfactorily explained in terms of human genius alone? The traditional answers of Judaism and Christianity have been that the Bible—defined, of course, differently by the two communities —was given by God, that the human writers played only a secondary part. If this postulate is granted, a number of questions follow concerning the relationship between divine author and human amanuensis.

The word 'inspiration' means 'in-breathing' and, though the root is Latin, the figure is Hebraic. On the day of creation God breathed into the lifeless form of man and he became a 'living soul' (Gen. 2.7). The word for 'breath' or 'spirit' (Hebrew *ruach*), so important in this discussion, does not occur in this verse. However, though its absence is striking, the idea is in line with all those many passages where *ruach* does occur, as, for example, Ezek. 37, where the wind blows into dead bodies and they live.

Ruach originally meant 'wind' and it provided the Hebrew with the ideal image for God, because the wind was invisible, intangible, uncontrollable, unpredictable and devastating. Man had some vestigial *ruach* of his own; he could puff and blow, even if his breath could not flatten the harvest. There were also times of great excitement, when breath came in great gulps and man was able to perform remarkable feats. The connection between high achievement and heavy breathing seemed obvious, and an explanation was offered in terms of the breath of God blowing into man and increasing his vital power. So in Judges we read of the spirit (or breath) of God coming on Samson,

43

enabling him to tear a lion into pieces and do other supra-normal things (14.6,19; 15.14). This is a far cry from what we mean by inspiration, but the Samson story gives the genesis of the idea. Two important elements are established—the unlimited power of the spirit on one hand, and the point of contact and communion on the other.

In time it became clear that the entry of the divine into the human need not be associated with fleeting, dramatic and mainly physical feats of strength. The Bible begins to talk about the spirit of God bringing more permanent gifts. The concrete factor of divine power entering by the breath was lost, but the same language was used. Bezalel, the priestly architect, was full of the divine spirit, but the exercise of his gifts is not normally associated with vigorous respiration (Exod. 31.3). As the concrete element receded, the personal relationship developed. No longer was it the breath of God blowing into man's lungs but the spirit of God communing with man's spirit. It is sometimes difficult to say whether *ruach* represents impersonal, divine power or a personal spirit; and in the case of man, whether it represents the phsyical capacity to inhale divine breath or a distinct element in personality which renders man capable of communion with God. By the time we come to Paul, the matter is fully worked out. God's spirit meets with the spirit of the believer and creates in him new faculties of prophecy, tongues, healing, faith, meekness, and so on (1 Cor. 12.4–11).

It is on this biblical basis that Jewish and Christian notions of inspiration are constructed. The problem is: when the divine Spirit enters fallible man, thus inspiring him, is human fallibility overcome?

This question would not be easy to answer even if there were no complicating factors, but there is one such factor of great importance. Few biblical books had an author in the simple sense of the term. Paul's letters had, but the same does not apply to the Synoptic Gospels nor to most of the books of the Old Testament. Literary studies lead to the conclusion that the process of composition of a typical Old Testament book was as follows:

  a. groups of unknown people composed oral forms to help
     them with their work, their worship, their teaching;

b. the oral forms were passed on through the generations, undergoing small changes from time to time;

c. local men of letters wrote down the oral forms with which they were familiar;

d. in some period of great literary activity, an editor collected these various literary products and combined them in one large work;

e. the large work might be combined with others to make up a complete roll.

That is not a simple process; nevertheless, in the case of some books, it must be a greatly simplified account. As far as the prophetic books are concerned, the first stage needs to be modified to make room for the supremely creative figure and his disciples, but the rest of the process holds. In the New Testament we have to think of decades rather than generations, but otherwise the process is much the same. The relevance of this to the question of inspiration is clear. Can a notion of inspiration be devised that takes account of this large army of contributors?

Some interpreters refuse to reckon with this problem, arguing that each biblical book had one specific author. Moses wrote the Pentateuch, Isaiah wrote Isaiah, Matthew wrote Matthew, and so on. Some problems are removed by this hypothesis, but others remain and are aggravated. There is no space to treat this view in detail, but much of what is said in the latter part of this chapter bears upon it.

One common way of tackling the question is to put the Bible on a par with other literary works and to see it as the product of religious genius. There are people, never more than a few in any generation, who stand out from the mass by virtue of exceptional talent. These precious few have something which can reasonably be called genius. Furthermore, none of us, whether genius or journeyman, works always on the same level. There are times when we produce work that is far beyond our normal expectation. When these two factors operate together, the unique work is born. Inspiration, it is sometimes said, means simply that. It is a way of describing what happens when an exceptionally gifted person has moments of supreme insight.

45

This is a humanistic—though it may also be a devout—approach to the problem. Inspiration of this kind, however, belongs to every form of human endeavour. Setting the fourth Gospel alongside *King Lear* is not without problems, but if the language of inspiration is to be used of a speech in the House of Commons, or an article in *Punch*, or even a three-set victory at Wimbledon, one begins to wonder if anything really serious is being said at all. The excellent performance is rare, but it is to be found in every area of human activity. If a dramatist can be a genius, so can a ballet-dancer, and so can a jockey. Is not the Bible demeaned when its inspiration is discussed against this background?

It can be argued that the Bible retains its dignity because of its matter. A great statesman is more significant than a great batsman, because statesmanship is more significant than batting. The Bible is concerned not with a trivial end like scoring runs or even negotiating treaties, nor simply with the human condition, as a drama might be, but with the whole truth about God and his ways with men. Inspiration that relates to that supreme subject is inspiration indeed. There is, therefore, no need to posit a special mechanism of inspiration in relation to the Bible. When exalted human genius is addressed to such profound matters, the dignity of the Bible is secure.

On this reckoning there is no difficulty regarding the army of contributors, for the whole process is explained in terms of natural function. Nor do the obvious limits of the Bible as a cultural artefact create a problem, since one would expect a human creation to show the marks of its context.

It remains to ask what place is left for divine activity in this account of biblical inspiration. The answer must be that God was not immediately responsible for the writings of the biblical authors, but, in that he is creator of all things, the giver of talents, the inspirer of all good men, his place is clear though distant. He is the origin of the prophetic gift and the prophetic vision. He is the instigator of prophetic activity. But that is all. Within this framework the prophet exercises his gifts with human freedom amid human limitations. That, so it is said, is consistent with the actual appearance of the biblical books.

Numerous criticisms have been made of this view of inspiration; the most serious is that it takes no account of the fact of evil in human affairs. Heightened faculties produce not only great works of art but great wickedness. The most spectacular example in this century of the impact made by a man of talent rising above himself was the Nuremberg rallies. Are we to say that Hitler was inspired? If not, what force does the word 'inspiration' have? Good men in their supreme moments are inspired. Bad men are not, but seem to be equally effective. Is it sufficient to reply that bad men have never given us anything to compare with the Bible?

At the other extreme is the notion of mechanical inspiration. God overruled the human agents so that they became automata and produced books that were free from error, touched, but unspoilt, by human hand. To a large extent this view exists only in the imagination of those who attack it. Words like 'mechanical' and 'automata' are not words that one applies to oneself. No one with much theological sense would talk about God working mechanically. There is little need, therefore, to spend time discussing mechanical inspiration. This does not rule out other positive and vigorous notions that have been current for centuries. They merit most careful consideration.

Authorship can be understood in two senses. The stress may be laid on the actual writing or on the origin, the fount and source of the ideas. Some interpreters distinguish between the two and attribute the latter to God and the former to man. Seen as literature, the Bible shows every sign of multiplicity of authorship because the contributors were human and there were many of them. But overall the Bible shows a constant purpose, to record and expound God's activity in the world. The unity in the Bible is due to its single, divine author. There is no contradiction between the two.

Neither is there contradiction between God's work in creation which endows men with natural talents and the work of inspiration that provides those talents with their supreme opportunity. Extremists on both sides have argued as if belief in one ruled out the other. If God gave men talents in creation, special inspiration was unnecessary; or, if God inspired man, his natural ability was unimportant. Both these contentions set up an absurd dichotomy within the divine activity. The view of inspiration with which we are now concerned does not make this mistake. It neither pushes God away into the distance nor does violence

47

to human nature. It holds that there is an essential difference between man's ordinary work and his inspired work, but that there is continuity between them.

The passionate speech of a sensitive and gifted man is a most persuasive force. The way in which it differs from inspired speech is critical for the view we are now investigating. Men of all kinds can be passionate and sensitive and gifted, but only in certain particular places and at certain particular times were men inspired. The Bible, unlike *King Lear*, is the result of specific and direct inspiration. God is author, in the sense of fount and origin; he communicates to the human authors truths not available to them by the exercise of their own faculties. Man's participation, however, means that the writing is expressed through the medium of the writer's culture.

There are various points that can be set against this argument. Does it suggest mechanical control? No, because all that is said of the human authors is that they were enabled to grasp truths that, in their normal capacity, they could not grasp. This does not turn men into machines but simply reverses the effects of the Fall and makes the writers momentarily into true human beings. Does it rest on a circular argument? To some extent, yes. Belief in inspiration rests on what the Bible says and the Bible is trusted because it is inspired. This criticism is allayed by marshalling other, non-biblical arguments for the inspiration of the Bible. What of the errors in the Bible? Inspiration does not guarantee every word. The writers were free to make their own mistakes and to introduce their own irrelevancies. In the case of some odd facts the Bible may be wrong, but this does not matter. In the great truths of man's salvation it is not wrong.

What of the argument raised above regarding the large number of people engaged in composing the Bible? This is more difficult. Some of them can be ignored on the grounds that all authors have sources and that it is what authors do with sources that makes literature. Inspiration, therefore, need be related only to the key figures. This does not solve the question of translation. Are all translators inspired? It might have been easier to assert this in the days before the market was flooded with Bibles. Today the very success of the Bible makes the contention more difficult.

In summary, there is a wide divergence of opinion regarding inspiration. There are some who see the Bible as a great book, but who do not regard it as the consequence of divine action. For these people, the word 'inspiration' is a metaphor. Those who take a theological view, but who see God everywhere and in everything, will see the Bible as part of the great literature of the world but superior to it in degree. The word 'inspiration' is no metaphor, but they think of it in general rather than particular terms. Those who take a more transcendental view, who accept a supernatural activity of God in the world as well as a natural one, will see inspiration as a series of specific divine acts by means of which particular people were moved to write.

9

THE CANON

If a collection of writings is inspired and held in reverence by a religious community, it must be possible to define it precisely. Sacred books must not have indeterminate limits. Sacredness implies separation; sacred places, sacred vessels, sacred persons are distinguished from other places, vessels and persons. It follows that any ascription to the Bible of a special quality will imply a clear definition of what the Bible is. The world will want to know which words have this quality and which do not.

In the first place we need to consider the books of the Old Testament. The first five, Genesis, Exodus, Leviticus, Numbers and Deuteronomy, reached their final form in Hebrew about 400 B.C. and thereafter became the cornerstone of Judaism. The prophetic books followed some two centuries later, though they never acquired the authority that the Torah had and has for Judaism. The prophetic books are Joshua, Judges, Samuel and Kings—known since the eighth century A.D. as the Former Prophets—as well as Isaiah, Jeremiah, Ezekiel and the Twelve—known as the Latter Prophets, though the distinction between them does not belong to primitive Judaism. The Twelve are Hosea, Joel, Amos, Obadiah, Jonah, Micah, Nahum, Habakkuk, Zephaniah, Haggai, Zechariah and Malachi. The third section of the Hebrew Bible is the Writings and comprises Psalms, Job, Proverbs, the Five Rolls—Ruth, Song of Songs, Ecclesiastes, Lamentations and Esther—Daniel, Ezra-Nehemiah and Chronicles. This list contains the same books as are found in the AV, though the order is different, and the AV sometimes divides books that are not divided in the Hebrew.

By traditional reckoning the books of the Hebrew canon are twenty-four in number: five of Torah, eight of Prophets, and eleven of Writings. These are the books that 'render the hands unclean', that is to say, that are governed by special rules of holiness. The final number was arrived at only gradually; there was some dispute about Ecclesiastes and Song of Songs and perhaps other books as well.[1] It seems probable that a meeting of rabbis at Jamnia (Jabneh) after the fall of Jerusalem in A.D. 70 gave formal assent to this list, though there is no direct evidence. Josephus, writing around the year A.D. 100, refers to the three sections of the Hebrew canon, but by grouping the books differently he makes the total number twenty-two.[2] It is clear, then, not only that the Old Testament was given to the world by Israel, but also that its contents were determined by Jews alone. These contents have never been questioned.

The same conclusion does not hold for the Apocrypha. From the third century B.C. onwards the Hebrew books were translated into Greek for the benefit of Jews who lived outside the Holy Land. These Jews of the Diaspora added other books of their own. The Greek canon of the Old Testament is, therefore, larger than the Hebrew, and broadly speaking the difference is what we call the Apocrypha. In its early days Christianity flourished among Jews of the Diaspora and the Church took over the Septuagint, as the Greek Old Testament was called, and even added to it. Judaism repudiated it and produced other Greek versions for its own use.

It is evident then that a certain ambivalence attaches to the Apocrypha from the beginning. The primitive Church had trouble making up its mind. The Apocrypha was used in church but Jerome refused to regard it as canonical. Augustine, on the other hand, made no distinction between Apocrypha and Old Testament. The dispute rumbled on until the Reformation, when Luther categorically rejected the Apocrypha. The Council of Trent responded by including the Apocrypha firmly in the canon. The Church of England, ever in pursuit of the *via media*, affirmed in Article VI that these books 'the Church doth read for example of life and instruction of manners; but yet doth it not apply them to establish any doctrine'. Nothing could better illustrate the problem with which this chapter is concerned. Is there a clearly

[1] See the Jewish tractate 'Yadaim' (3.5), which is to be found in H. Danby, ed., *The Mishnah* (Oxford University Press 1933), pp. 781f.
[2] See *Flavius Josephus against Appion* (1.8).

defined Bible? Does it matter if some books appear to be half in and half out?

The situation today is much clearer. The Roman Catholic Jerusalem Bible includes the books of the Apocrypha scattered about within it. But, as biblical scholars have come to realize the importance of the Apocrypha for understanding both Judaism and Christianity, it is now normally included as a separate section in non-Catholic Bibles. This tidies up the problem as far as publishing is concerned, but it leaves us with tantalizing questions about the relative authority of different parts of holy writ.

The existence of a canon of Scripture in Judaism and its regular use in worship had considerable influence on primitive Christianity. From earliest times the Church made use of lections in worship and soon assembled its own literature to be read alongside the Old Testament. Literary production, however, was under no one's control. Not only Paul could write letters. A Christian literature emerged that included not only the Pauline epistles and the four Gospels but also fanciful works that enjoyed great popularity at least in their places of origin. During the second century, Gnosticism, a strange religious philosophy which blended all religions into one by means of the wildest speculations, was making rapid progress and producing a considerable literature of a quasi-Christian kind. If at this point the Christian Church had not been able to define its own writings, it would have been swamped.

Curiously the first hint of a solution to the Church's problem came from the heretic Marcion, who is often suspected of Gnostic leanings. He produced a canon to satisfy his own anti-Jewish notion of Christianity. It consisted of an edited version of Luke and ten Pauline letters. Before long more comprehensive lists appeared including those writings that could be attributed either to the apostles themselves or to their immediate disciples. In this way Christian orthodoxy was anchored to the teaching of the first few decades. Soon two notional lists emerged, one of generally acknowledged books—the four Gospels, Acts, the letters of Paul —and one of disputed books. Hebrews, James, 2 Peter, 2 and 3 John, Jude and Revelation were all disputed at some time, while the Shepherd of Hermas, the Epistle of Barnabas and 1 Clement had their defenders. The list of the twenty-seven books that now make up the New Testament first appears in the Festal Letter of Athanasius in the year A.D. 376. Confirmation comes from a council held in Rome under Damasus in 382 and the Synod of Carthage, 397. Some discussion continued in the West, but the contents page of the New Testament has never been seriously challenged since the end of the fourth century.

Fixing the canon settles the major problem of defining what the Bible actually is, but that is not quite the end of the story. One tends to talk about individual books as if they were absolute and unalterable documents, but this is far from true. Those who possess Bibles with 'marginal readings' will have noticed that footnotes often suggest different translations. Occasionally the footnote says, 'Many ancient authorities read ...' and there follow a few words that may be quite different in sense from what is in the main text. The reason for these footnotes is simple. The earliest manuscripts of the Bible are very old, sometimes mutilated, and often unclear. Moreover they differ. They differ because copyists never were perfect and, even with the oldest of our manuscripts, there must have been several stages of copying between the original document and the one we possess. Discrepancies between manuscripts are rarely large, though there is a famous problem about the proper ending of Mark's Gospel and a great deal of uncertainty about the story of the woman taken in adultery in John 7.53—8.1. But if the discrepancies are not large, they are certainly numerous. There are thousands of minute variations between texts and, every time a new manuscript is discovered, the number increases. When the Isaiah scroll from Qumran was first read in 1947, it added hundreds of variations to that book alone. Rarely are these variations significant for the meaning of the text. Often they merely affect spelling and grammar. But they exist, a clear testimony to the fact that ancient scribes, highly professional though they might have been, were only human.

This discussion leads to certain conclusions. In the first place, any attempt to delineate the Bible with absolute precision is bound to fail. Although some, both Jews and Christians, attempt to do just this, it is hard to follow their argument through. One may take the Bible with the utmost seriousness, but to contend that, letter by letter, it descended from God is scarcely possible. Nor is it of any avail to quote Matt. 5.18. The statement that no jot or tittle will pass from the Law before the end is, alas, hyperbole, for every textual critic knows that that is exactly what many jots and tittles have done.

Secondly, and on the other hand, a reasonable argument can be put forward that the Bible enshrines a complete rule of faith and life. Both Jews and Christians make such a claim. Thus the Bible exercises a continuing control over the historical community, and, because the Bible is now fixed, the community will be held fast to its original basis.

Thirdly, many fallible men and many fallible institutions have played some part in the Bible's emergence and transmission. Protestants stand in debt to Catholics and Catholics to Jews, and perhaps we all stand in debt to the Jacobean Anglicans who gave us the AV. This is a happy thought, for it represents an unrealized and inevitable ecumenism.

Lastly, it needs to be stressed that synods and councils played only a minor role. The canon was not established by authority. Nothing was confirmed until the general usage made the confirmation a formality. The common mind of believers gave us both testaments, and the vast influence of the Bible today is a witness not to the perspicacity of ecclesiastical gatherings, but to the vitality of the religious life of Jewish and Christian communities.

PART 2

APPROACHES

10

THE USE OF THE OLD TESTAMENT
IN THE PRIMITIVE CHURCH

So far this book has been concerned with the issues that arise when one attempts to read the Bible as a book having relevance to the present day. It is now necessary to be constructive, that is to say, to give an account of various ways in which the Bible is expounded to bring out its contemporary relevance. Each of the following chapters is concerned with an approach which its exponents regard as the only proper approach to the interpretation of the Bible. We begin with the primitive Church and its Scriptures.

Christianity began as an offshoot of Judaism. Whatever may have been the case later on, the earliest Christian preachers and their audiences shared the same Jewish inheritance. The earliest disputes were internal Jewish affairs, Jews contending with Jews about the Messiah. The issue was a contentious one. All Jews agreed that God had called Abraham out of Ur, that he had made a special choice of Israel, raised up Moses to be a deliverer, revealed the Holy Law on Sinai, sealed a covenant with his people, led them to the promised land, sent them David and the prophets and guided them through history giving them prosperity and chastisement in due measure. As promise after promise seemed to be fulfilled, the Jewish people became ever more confident that the greatest of all promises would be honoured. Israel would be finally released from all who afflicted her and, purified by strict judgement, would at last enjoy the new age. Up to this point Christian Jews and non-Christian Jews were in agreement; but then the Christians went a step further. They said that God had revealed his hand again, that the long-awaited deliverer had arrived, and that he was Jesus of Nazareth.

Most Jews rejected this proposition. Jesus did not fit the

57

picture. He was no triumphant conqueror: he left the situation much as he found it, and he died a criminal's death, bringing upon himself the curse of the Law. His death was no martyrdom in the cause of Israel, for he died as a blasphemer condemned by Jewish authorities, not as a rebel under the sentence of Rome.

This represented a formidable case for the Christians to answer and it soon became even more difficult. While official Judaism repudiated Jesus, certain Gentiles acknowledged him—first devout men like Cornelius, who were impressed with the Jewish faith, and then others, some with dubious religious backgrounds. What, then, of God's purpose in history? Those who possessed the Law had rejected the promised deliverer; those who knew nothing of Law or promise accepted him. That was the Christian affirmation. To Jews it was the ultimate blasphemy because it made God look foolish.

The only thing the Christians could do was to try to prove their case by traditional Jewish methods. Making use of the sacred books of Jewish history, they tried to argue that Jesus was the Messiah. In Judaea, Syria, Asia Minor, Greece and eventually in Rome itself, the debate went on. Acts concludes with Paul's arrival in Rome, where he met the Jewish elders and tried to convince them about Jesus both from the Law of Moses and from the prophets (Acts 28.23).

The first step in understanding Christian interpretation is, therefore, to take a look at Jewish interpretation, because Judaism provided the context, the method and the style of the argument.

Long before the Christian era Judaism had made up its mind about the Torah. As delivered to Moses it was the perfect and final Word of God. Every syllable carried the authority of God himself. The Prophets and the Writings, though not themselves Torah, were but a little way behind, since they expounded Torah and never departed from it.

There was general agreement in the first century that prophecy had ceased with Haggai and Zechariah and that, therefore, there would be no new biblical books. Israel, however, was not left to face new crises without any divine word to support her. Because the Scriptures contained the perfect revelation, they were relevant to every conceivable situation. All that was necessary was to study the text diligently enough to bring out the divine guidance hidden in it.

For this reason Jewish interpreters distinguished two meanings in the Scriptures, one plain and available to all, the other secret and available only to those who could see beneath the surface. The plain meaning was limited in that it was inflexible; the words had the same sense from generation to generation. But the secret meaning, though based on the traditional text, could be inferred to suit the moment. It could claim both topicality and supreme authority. If one asks how the secret meaning was discovered in writing that had been unchanged for centuries, the answer is— by a rigorous process of deduction carried out in humble and openly confessed dependence on divine grace. That was the formula. It made possible a new industry in Judaism. Textually corrupt passages could be made to yield impressive secret meanings, and large interpretative edifices could be built on small foundations.

This kind of exegesis allowed the imagination free rein. Odd words provided pages of exposition. There was less and less need to consider the text as a whole. But the process was not simply a free-for-all. The rabbis were devout men, much concerned about the validity of their deductions. They discussed interpretations endlessly. Idiosyncratic conclusions were ruled out. In the course of time complex systems of interpretation were worked out, so that the soundness of any particular conclusion could be assessed, at least by experts. The discussion continued. The interpretations multiplied. The task became more and more technical. Behind it all the absolute authority of the Torah was never for a moment impaired.

Against this background the infant Church set about convincing the Jewish world that Jesus was the Messiah. There were two sides to the argument. On one hand it was axiomatic that, if the purpose of God extended to a crucified Messiah, that unlooked-for truth would be securely, if secretly, locked up in Scripture. Discontinuity between Scripture and Messiah was unthinkable. Dislocation in Israel's divinely ordained progress through history was equally unacceptable. The Christian apologist, therefore, had to comb the Scriptures to find passages that, faithfully studied, yielded the truth that Jesus was the fulfilment of messianic expectation and the infant Church the extension of

Israel's historic identity. If he failed, the argument was lost before it was begun. On the other hand, Christians had also to substantiate a bolder claim. They asserted that Jesus had not merely fulfilled the Scriptures but transcended them. In his life, death and resurrection a new age had begun, making the former age with its conventions, values and even its Torah old. In the new age there was a new divine community and a new way to God. The Scriptures foretold the new age, but Jesus embodied it, so that, in the last resort, all authorities had to bow to him.

There is an element of paradox in this: the fulfilment of the Law and the end of the Law, Jesus attested by Scripture but supreme above Scripture. It cannot have been an easy case to argue. The question naturally arises: who first worked it out? At one time Paul was given the credit, but increasingly scholars find themselves coming back to the proposition that no rabbi could have promulgated such a novel doctrine. So, despite all the difficulties of establishing what he actually said and did, attention is turning more and more to Jesus himself. Is the Christian argument, the argument that went beyond skilful use of words and texts, that asserted what had never been asserted before, the argument that Scripture was surpassed—not denied but extended—and that the text must give way to the living Word, to be directly attributed to Jesus? It is hard to appreciate how revolutionary this assertion was. In Judaism the Torah was the inexhaustible fountain, the Word to which Israel would never turn in vain. In Christian interpretation Torah and Prophets witnessed to Jesus. The transfiguration narrative, in which Jesus appears in glory with the great law-giver and the great prophet as supporters, says it all. Law and Prophets are witnesses, but Jesus stands on a different plane (Mark 9.2–8).

It is not difficult to find examples of Christian writers using the Old Testament in a thoroughly Jewish way. The first thing to notice is the abundance of Old Testament quotations in the New Testament. Jesus constantly cites the Old Testament. So does Paul. Paul supplies a fine example of the use of secret meaning in a dispute he was having with the Corinthians about his apostleship and the rights of maintenance that were associated with that status. He quotes what was to him the Mosaic Law, 'You shall not muzzle an ox when it treads out the grain' (Deut. 25.4) and continues, 'Is it for oxen that God is concerned?

Does he not speak entirely for our sake?' (1 Cor. 9.9). So Deuteronomy's concern for oxen is turned into an argument that hard-working Christian preachers should have a right to financial support. This is typical of the rabbis' style of argument, which often proceeded on the principle: 'If this is true and stated in the Law, then how much more true is that.'

Matthew's Gospel does something similar in the infancy narrative. In a moving passage in Hosea the prophet had recalled God's deep love for Israel in its earliest days as a nation. 'When Israel was a child, I loved him, and out of Egypt I called my son' (Hosea 11.1). The narrative in Matthew tells of Joseph and Mary returning to the Holy Land after the death of Herod, and the parallel proves irresistible (Matt. 2.15). 'Out of Egypt I called my son.' Secretly and unknowingly Hosea was speaking of Jesus. In Luke's account of the sermon on the day of Pentecost Peter applies the same method to Ps. 16. The psalmist expresses his confidence in God. 'Thou dost not give me up to Sheol, or let thy godly one see the Pit.' Is the psalmist speaking of his own experience? Not as far as Peter is concerned. David— the assumed author—died. He *did* see the pit. So the words cannot apply to him. They therefore relate to Jesus and the resurrection (Acts 2.25–32). Arguments of this kind, although making a thoroughly Christian point, are pursuing a normal Jewish method. The sacred text has secret meaning. Devout insight, faithfully pursued, can reveal what that meaning is.

This is not the heart of the matter. The manifold use of Old Testament quotations is significant. The Jewish style is interesting but hardly surprising. The point that demands attention, however, is the christological content of the argument. The Christian apologist was really saying that the whole Old Testament, not simply odd words and phrases, but the whole sacred text and the history that lay behind it, pointed to Jesus. Inerrant as the Law might be, the Old Testament Scriptures were not final. They were full of expectation, and the Christian affirmation set out conveniently by Mark as the first words of Jesus' ministry was, 'The time is fulfilled, and the kingdom of God is at hand' (Mark 1.15).

Others in Judaism had been bold enough to say that the last days, referred to by prophets and apocalyptists, were already present. Christianity said more: that all the prophecies came into focus in the life and ministry of Jesus. This was a claim of breathtaking audacity. The Scriptures pointed to *him*! The early Church had no doubts on the point. The miracle stories are related as signs that the last days had arrived. The resurrection was cited as proof that the new age had begun. Scripture was quoted whenever possible to force the message home.

Many examples can be found to make this point. None can be traced back to Jesus with absolute confidence, but the hypothesis that the originality is his has no more difficulties than any other. Luke reports that when Jesus came to the synagogue of Nazareth, he read from Isa. 61.1, 'The Spirit of the Lord God is upon me ...' and then continued, 'Today this scripture has been fulfilled in your hearing' (Luke 4.21). This is not simply an argument from Scripture to a situation where the words could be made to fit. It is an argument from a position of authority back to a supporting witness. It is possible only because Christians saw Jesus as the one through whom the last days had come. Similarly in Mark 12.10, Jesus asserts that, within the paradoxical ways of God, the chosen Son himself can be rejected by men, like the stone, ignored by the builders, that eventually becomes the head of the corner. This use of Ps. 118 can be understood only as an affirmation that every secret allusion in Scripture establishes the sonship of Jesus. Again in Mark 12.35, Jesus attacks the common expectation that a Son of David would restore the empire on the grounds that David in Ps. 110 refers to the coming one as his lord. David would never have called a descendant lord. So the coming one was not to be recognized simply as a son of David but as a figure with greater than royal attributes. The argument rests on an uncritical approach to the Psalter and to Davidic authorship, but, be that as it may, it makes sense only upon the lips of one about whom the most exalted claims were made.

These are but three examples of many. The use of messianic titles, the performance of messianic actions, the reference at the Last Supper to 'the new covenant in my blood', which echoes Jeremiah—these and many other pieces of evidence show that the New Testament interpretation of the Old was little concerned with finding new applications for the timeless words and much concerned to show that, in whole and in part, the Old

Testament looked to Jesus, and Jesus alone provided its ultimate meaning.

The significant fact, therefore, is not that Christian interpretation had something in common with Pharisaic methods, but that, while the Pharisees were concerned with the Torah, Christian interpretation proclaimed Jesus as the Word of God beyond the Law. Perhaps the clearest guide is the curious form of words with which Jesus begins his speeches: 'Truly, truly, I say to you ...' The implication is unmistakable: 'It is I who speak, not the ancient Law'. To paraphrase Mark 1.22, he taught as one who had authority *in himself* and not as the scribes who referred back constantly to the Law. In Matthew's Sermon on the Mount the case is made more explicit. The Law is cited several times and then taken a stage further, not in rabbinic fashion to defend the Law and prevent it from being broken by accident, but as an actual higher command supported only by the personal authority of Jesus. This is a profound departure from Jewish understanding as well as from Jewish methods.

The early Christian preachers did not, therefore, begin with the Torah. They began with Jesus. Their faith was focused on the person; only in relation to that person did they make use of the sacred writings that preceded him.

This is the point of departure for all Christian interpretation of the Bible. There now exist two Testaments, an Old, which represents expectation, and a New, which witnesses to fulfilment. In the course of time the two have become the Bible, and the Bible exists in the Christian Church as a clearly defined text. Is it possible for the wheel to turn the full circle and for Christians to approach their text much as the Pharisee approached his? If that were to happen, the distinctive element in the New Testament would be lost. New Testament Christianity is a faith in a living person, an incarnate, crucified, risen and reigning Lord. Christians encounter him by faith. For them the Word has become flesh. As long as Scripture, old and new, points them to that Jesus who is known by faith, Christian believers will be standing on New Testament ground. Problems of interpretation there will certainly be, but the questions will be seen in the right perspective. To some extent the whole story of Christian interpretation has to do with this problem: how to relate the text and the person.

11

ALLEGORY

Interpretation is concerned with language, the language of the text and the language of the interpreter and his audience. Language is a subtle tool. At one end of the spectrum it is precise, it can state a case with perfect clarity; at the other end it is profound and allusive, it can throw up images and stimulate feeling on such a scale that no one, not the author, not the reader, can say what the full import of the writing is. Figurative language is essentially open-ended. Legal documents are free from figures. Poetry is full of them.

Literary figures are of various kinds. There are similes, metaphors, proverbs, parables, where the figure is expressed in a brief story, literary symbols, like heaven and hell—when they are used non-technically—and so on. And there are allegories. It would be useful to establish some kind of definition of allegory, but figurative speech is not patient of exact analysis. This is particularly true with regard to the Bible, where figurative speech abounds and where two Hebrew terms, *mashal* and *hidah*, are used to cover parable, metaphor, allegory, proverb and everything else. The clearest example of an allegory in the Old Testament, Ezek. 17, is described as both a *mashal* and a *hidah*.

What then is an allegory? It usually takes the form of a narrative, often a bizarre narrative making no pretensions to verisimilitude, a narrative which is, in fact, an extended metaphor expounding a series of abstract truths by means of symbolic elements in the story. An eagle comes to Lebanon and takes the topmost branch off a cedar tree and carries it away to plant it in a foreign land. In place of the cedar the eagle plants a vine. Another eagle appears and the vine 'bent its roots towards him'. That is the message of Ezek. 17. This particular allegory is easy enough to decode. The eagles are the Babylonian king Nebuchadnezzar and the Egyptian Pharaoh, Lebanon is Jerusalem, the two trees are Jehoiachin and Zedekiah. The situation fits the year 588 B.C., when Jehoiachin was carried into exile and Zedekiah, set up as a vassal of Babylon, had foolishly begun to intrigue with Egypt. The narrative, therefore, proves to be a prophetic denunciation of Zedekiah for breaking his agreement with Babylon and treacherously turning to Egypt. The point might have been put more clearly, but in Hebrew eyes the *mashal* had a dignity that blunt statements lacked.

There are differences between the allegory and the parable, especially the New Testament parable. In the first place, the parable is usually a simple, credible story. It is usually fiction, but it belongs to the realm of common experience and something like it could happen. On the other hand, the allegory is a contrived and often absurd story leaving the reader who cannot see beneath the surface bewildered. There is a reason for the difference. The parable is concerned to make a single point, or two or three points closely related to each other. The whole story revolves around this point and the details have no significance except to make the story more interesting. In the course of time other points may be added to a parable, as for example in the parable of the Marriage Feast (Matt. 22.1–14), but this means a departure from the pure parabolic form. The point of the parable of the Good Samaritan was that virtue sometimes rested in the despised foreigner rather than in the technically pure officials of Judaism. Jerusalem, Jericho, the thieves, the donkey, the inn, the twopence, these appear simply to make a good story. In allegory every detail is significant. The eagles, Lebanon, the branch, the vine are symbols and contribute to the meaning. This explains why allegories often have such a curious form. One cannot take the details of a complex situation, represent them all by symbols, and work all the symbols into a simple narrative. There is something frank and open about the parable. New Testament parables often begin, 'The kingdom of heaven is like …', and there is little room for doubt about the didactic purpose. Occasionally an explanation appears, as in the case of the Sower in Mark 4, but the explanation is hardly necessary and is more problematic than the parable itself. The allegory, however, tends to be deliberately evasive. Its power lies in its mystery, as if the longer one needed to think about its sense, the more significant the sense would be in the end. There is, perhaps, another difference in that parables often have a concrete, practical purpose, whereas allegories are concerned with abstract and theoretical meaning. This is a generalization, but it helps to establish the difference in mood between the two literary forms.

Despite the differences parables and allegories cannot be clearly distinguished in the Bible. Some allegories are simple and short enough almost to be parables. Some parables grow more complex as they are applied in different circumstances.

So far we have considered only allegory written as allegory. Examples are found in Ezekiel and in the apocalyptic passages of such books as Daniel, Zechariah and Revelation. They present intricate problems of exegesis because the intent of the symbolic language is difficult to recover. Interpretation, in the sense in which the word is being used in this book, begins only when the deliberate allegories have been unravelled and the question of wider reference is raised. There is, however, a method of interpretation which proceeds by reading whole tracts of Scripture as allegory, *whether they were written in that literary form or not*. This method provides the real subject matter of this chapter. A clear distinction is therefore necessary between those biblical passages which the authors intended as allegory and those which some interpreters elect to read as allegory, whether they were originally meant to be allegory or not.

This method of interpretation, widespread in both Judaism and Christianity, is not as arbitrary as it sounds. It is based upon a profound respect for the text. If God is author, who can say with precision what his intent was? Does not God work miracles of communication through the text, so than no one can put a limit to the meaning of the simplest scriptural word? Does not the Bible go on being true for generation after generation in ways unthought of by author and interpreter alike? Those who ask such questions expect to find divine truth in every detail of a narrative, and they would allow no biblical exegete to tell them what the author's intention was. When the author is God, limiting statements about intention verge on blasphemy. This is the theological defence of the allegorical method.

For Christians there is the added fact that there are examples of the method in the New Testament itself. Paul knew that, according to Gen. 16 and 21, Abraham had two sons, one by a serving maid and called Ishmael, and one by Sarah, his wife, and called Isaac. These things, says Paul in Gal. 4, are an allegory, for the two women are two covenants bearing children for bondage or for freedom. In 1 Cor. 10 allegory and typology are mixed together. Typology is a way of seeing events of the Old Testament as forerunners and anticipations of definitive events in the New. Here the crossing of the Red Sea is seen as a type of baptism. Paul speaks of spiritual food and spiritual drink in the wilderness as a type of the Eucharist and continues in allegorical style with the statement, 'and the rock was Christ'. The story in question is found in Exod. 17. Moses, embarrassed by the complaints of the thirsty Israelites, was told to smite the rock, and water flowed out (see also Num. 20.1–13). If a sharp distinction is made between typology and allegory, there is an abrupt change in 1 Cor. 10 as Paul moves from events that *prefigure* Christian sacraments to a detail that *signifies* Christ. It is hardly possible that Paul was aware of making such a change. He was simply using Jewish language in a Jewish way.

Because it has been maintained that Christianity borrowed the allegorical method exclusively from the Greeks, passing reference must be made to Jewish allegorists. The probable pioneer was one Aristobulus, who wrote in the second century B.C. an exposition of the Mosaic Law which unfortunately is known to us only through citations in other writers. His home was Alexandria, and he was able to read such deep philosophical truth in the works of Moses that he claimed that all Greek philosophers found their ideas in the Mosaic Law. The Letter of Aristeas (*c.* 100 B.C.) is also concerned to see profound reason in the Mosaic Law.[1] Permission to eat animals that have cloven hooves and chew the cud, which is granted in Lev. 11.3, is explained as an exhortation to particular virtues. The division of the hoof represents discrimination, on which the whole weight of virtue rests. Chewing the cud represents memory, reflection, the calling of divine events back to the mind. No doubt there is Greek influence here, but before launching into a study of the

[1] The Letter of Aristeas is to be found in, R. H. Charles, ed., *The Apocrypha and Pseudepigrapha of the Old Testament*, vol. 2 (Oxford University Press 1913), pp. 94ff. See verses 150–2.

Hellenistic background it is well to remember that Jewish writers also practised the art.

Allegorical interpretation is said to have been invented in the centuries before the Christian era by Greek teachers to make Homer relevant and comprehensible in their own generation. The ancient poet was regarded in the fifth century B.C. as the fount of all wisdom regarding morals, philosophy, physics, medicine, gymnastics and everything else. Why his writing exercised this influence is hard to say. Edwin Hatch, in a famous book of the last century, attributed it to three things: the glamour that surrounded the written word; the deep reverence felt for antiquity; and a positive belief that the words were divinely inspired.[2] The difficulty with Homer was that he was full of contradictions and, according to the sensibilities of later times, given to vulgarity and slack in his observations about the gods. How could one who was intrinsically so right be apparently so wrong? Faithful interpreters found the answer in the assumption that his writing was allegorical.

If all this is true, it is easy to see how Greek methods of dealing with Homer were transferred to the Bible. Jews and Christians had become students of philosophy. They, too, were exploring new avenues of human knowledge and understanding. Equally they were bound to a text they believed to have been written under direct inspiration. All truth was hidden therein. So the allegorists went to work, the literal meaning receded and secret meanings of ever-increasing complexities were extracted.

The first great exponent of the art of allegorizing the Bible was a Jew. He lived in Alexandria in the first century A.D. and was devoted to Greek philosophy and the Jewish Scriptures. He set out to demonstrate that his two enthusiasms were compatible. Philo is often called eclectic, which is unfair if the implication is that he picked from here and there without having absolute standards. For him the Scriptures were absolute. In them there was no contradiction, no confusion, no falsehood and nothing superfluous. Every line revealed its divine origin. What seemed confused or contradictory was the superficial, literal sense, not the true meaning. In a splendid piece of philosophizing Philo

[2] See E. Hatch, *The Influence of Greek Ideas on Christianity* (Harper and Row 1957), pp. 50f. This is a paperback edition of lectures delivered in 1888.

examines the statement, 'Cain went out from the face of God' (Gen. 4.16), and shows how thoroughly unsound its literal meaning was. God has no face—or he might be said to have other organs—and it is impossible to go away from the omnipresent. The statement is nonsense. It is redeemed when Cain is seen as the symbol of voluntary sin as opposed to Adam—*driven* out of the garden in Gen. 3.24—who symbolizes involuntary sin, less heinous and more amenable to cure.[3]

This is not exegesis as we understand it because it passes over the original meaning as of no account. It is, however, imaginative interpretation. Philo the Jew therefore poses the question that allegorical interpretation always raises. Is there one original and definitive meaning which should control all interpretation, or is meaning a function of the text that reveals itself in different ways in different places? Allegorical interpretation rests firmly on the second alternative.

Alexandria, Philo's home, was in the early Christian centuries a centre of learning second to none. A school of Christian theology was set up there at the end of the second century which aimed to do for Christianity what Philo had done for Judaism, that is to say, expound its teaching in terms of contemporary philosophy. The allegorical method was one of its weapons. Clement of Alexandria (*c.* 155–*c.* 220), one of the first great scholars of Christianity, was head of the school. He saw a distinction in Scripture analogous to the distinction between body and spirit. How little he thought of the bodily element is shown by the way he handled the miracles. He concentrated not on the fact, nor on the christological witness, but on the secret allusions that he saw in the text.

The greatest of Alexandrian interpreters, however, was Clement's pupil, Origen. He distinguished three meanings in Scripture, literal, moral and allegorical or spiritual, but his main concern was with the last. In keeping with the philosophical notions of his day, Origen maintained that all things existed on two levels of reality. There was the level of concrete, material existence, on which the thing in question was available to the senses, and there was the level of true being on which the thing

[3] Philo's argument is to be found in C. K. Barrett, *The New Testament Background: Selected Documents* (S.P.C.K. 1961), pp. 180f.

69

in question could be perceived in purest essence, free from the limitations of sense, but only by the most refined spiritual vision. The material served as a representation and symbol of the true. Everything in the universe had this double aspect, not least the Bible. Cloddish people read it superficially and grasped its outward meaning. Those with vision could elucidate the symbols and see into the heart of Scripture. Origen was an apologist for the Christian faith. He was aware that among the cloddish people who read the Old Testament and found it full of crudities, contradictions and dubious morality were many opponents of Christianity who were eager to make capital out of its weaknesses. Origen's reply was, in the first place, to recognize their difficulties. What man of sense could accept that three days of creation had run their course before there was a sun, moon and stars? How could Adam hide from God behind a tree? How could the devil show Jesus all the kingdoms of the world? Origen admitted that, if he had had only the literal sense of Scripture to rely on, he too would have been a sceptic; but awareness of the spiritual sense transformed his understanding. The difficulties in the literal sense, therefore, should act as a warning to the wise and an incitement to look beyond it.

The allegorical method was not universal in early Christianity. The school of Antioch showed more interest in the original meaning of the text and the history that lay behind it. None the less, allegorical interpretation found a place in medieval orthodoxy. From the time of Augustine onwards four senses were recognized in Scripture: the literal, which relates to what actually happened; the moral, which interprets the writing in terms of moral exhortation, much as a children's story may have a 'moral'; the allegorical, which reveals the true faith; and the anagogical, which sees Scripture as a symbolic account of heavenly realities. The last two come close together. Thomas Aquinas, the greatest of medieval theologians, accepted the four senses, but he held that everything necessary for faith was to be found in the literal sense alone. This is the answer to those who fear that the allegorical method multiplies fantasies and produces confusion. Aquinas brings every symbolic interpretation back to the test of the literal sense of Scripture. The literal sense exercises the control. The other senses stimulate imaginative understanding. The position adopted by Aquinas is held by many both in and outside the Roman Catholic Church today.

The Reformers rejected allegory and made much of the plain, straightforward meaning of Scripture. This is also true of what one might call classical Protestantism. It is interesting, however, that certain Protestant minorities have turned to the allegorical method to substantiate doctrines that are not otherwise well grounded in Scripture. The beasts of Rev. 13 probably refer to Roman emperors, and the author is patently allegorizing. There have been interpreters, however, who have allegorized the allegory and found that the beasts were Hitler and Stalin. By the same token, Rosh, Meshech and Tubal, proper names which appear—inaccurately as far as Rosh is concerned—in the RV of Ezek. 38.2, refer to Russia, Moscow and Tobolsk. A leaflet arrived in the post the other day affirming that the sheaf presented at barley harvest in Lev. 23 stood for Christ and the two loaves for the Church of the Sanctified, the dead and the living, baked with leaven—that is, with the Pentecost experience. So it goes on, a testimony not only to the powers of human ingenuity but to the influence exercised by the Bible over believers of every kind.

Allegorical interpretation rests on a profound respect for the biblical text and a desire to sort out its problems. The method is more concerned with the literary aspect of the Bible than with its history, but although interpreters of this kind often disparage the literal and historical sense, they do not reject it altogether. What they do is to raise new questions about the meaning of meaning. If an Old Testament story meant one thing to its original authors, another to those who celebrated it in the cult, another to those who read it in exile, another to Christians of the first generation who read it in the light of Christ, another to Origen, another to Augustine, another to modern Jews and another to modern Christians, what is the meaning of that story? Considerations of this kind give pause to those who are anxious to write off all allegorical interpretation as spurious.

At the same time the question of authenticity has to be raised. Allegorical interpretation, without any form of control, has led to the debasement of the method. Judaism exercised control by insisting that nothing could be argued from the text which contradicted the teaching of the Torah. Consistency was the controlling factor. The position of the Roman Catholic Church is not too dissimilar to this. The authority of the Church determines what is and what is not authentic interpretation. Self-appointed allegorizers, however, can claim little credibility. Their notions are not necessarily suspect on the grounds that they are stranger than those of the more orthodox but because they are individualist and arbitrary. They belong to private systems and have only private authority.

Allegorical interpretation is best seen as a kind of theological poetry. Doctrines are not based on the work of Gerard Manley Hopkins or T. S. Eliot or Charles Wesley, but those Catholics, Anglicans and Methodists who are slow to appreciate definitive, doctrinal constitutions may be stirred to theological understanding by such writers. So, too, the allegorists are not to be jettisoned because they exalt their own imagination but rather valued insofar as they stimulate ours.

12

THE AUTHORITY OF THE CHURCH

One of the basic questions of interpretation is: can the Bible
stand by itself? Can it speak clearly to every generation without
the aid of any external, governing authority? The question does
not suggest that exegesis is unnecessary. Literary, historical,
cultural, philological studies must be pursued unremittingly, and
fresh light can be thrown on the text from any of these directions
at any moment. But such studies clarify and illuminate what is
there already. They do not control the text. Our question concerns the necessity of an external authority to determine the way
in which the Bible is to be understood. Can a document that is
fixed, unaltered and therefore presumably static, speak significantly and consistently to every generation without the intervention of some authoritative person or persons to affirm what
its meaning is and how it is relevant?

So much depends upon the status the Bible is thought to have.
If we think of it as a library of human wisdom but not the
Word of God, there is no reason to posit any external authority
to control interpretation. The reader himself can determine what
significance and authority the biblical statements deserve. But
if we hold that the Bible has a message that is true for all men,
the need for some kind of governing interpretation becomes much
more evident. Every interpreter brings his own presuppositions
to his task and exercises his own imagination. If there is no
external authority, it is hard to see how the notion of an essential
message can survive. At best, it would seem, the essential message
will be confused by different apprehensions of it.

This question suggests another, more profound one. Religious
faith, both Jewish and Christian, expresses itself in a life, personal and communal, involving beliefs, morals, cultic acts, ways
of valuing, and so on. The Bible, on the other hand, is a text,
lively, eloquent, provoking, but a text, static and finite. Can the

book, standing alone, be the sole, effective and continuing inspiration of the life of faith in these communities? Does not Judaism require a coherent community through which the wisdom and truth of the Torah can be mediated and in which they are, to some extent, realized? Is not the same thing true of Christianity? Children discover devout ways of thinking, acting, worshipping and valuing from their parents and teachers long before they read the Bible with understanding. Adults conform to social and cultic patterns far more readily than they study Scripture. The Bible is not effective without the community. However true its message, the message means little unless it is expressed in everyday conversation and continually 'lived out' in everyday affairs. If the Bible rests in the believing community, that community is able to determine, to some extent, how the Bible is understood.

Further strength is given to this argument when we consider how the Testaments actually came into being. There was a people of Israel before there was a Mosaic Law, a worshipping community before there was a Psalter, a historical nation before there were prophets. In New Testament times the life of Jesus, the witness of the early Church, the preaching of Paul, all preceded the earliest writings. In each case it was in, through and for the communities that the writings came into being. In many cases the writings did not simply 'come into being'. The communities created the writings to satisfy their needs and then preserved and protected them. In some cases this was a matter of corporate memory—one thinks of the day-to-day laws of ancient Israel—but in others we have to posit careful and constant activity. Paul's letters were originally fragile sheets of papyrus. They would have cracked, rotted, faded and disappeared if devoted people had not treasured them, put them in safe places and assiduously copied them. So there would have been no Old Testament without the rabbinic assemblies and no New Testament without the Church. Furthermore, as we saw in chapter 9, the communities determined which books should be in the canon and which books should be out.

Not only did the religious communities, Jewish and Christian, precede, create, select and preserve their Scriptures, they also expressed and express them in their lives. There can be no wholly consistent interpretation apart from these communities.

74

But the argument must not be pressed too far. The communities were historically necessary. They were and are sensitive to the implications of Scripture. The practical experience of living by the book through the centuries led to much profound insight. But that is not the same thing as saying that their interpretation is true. Jews and Christians have devoted much time and study to the Hebrew Bible, but they arrive at profoundly different conclusions. If we are to think of interpretation as either true or false, both conclusions cannot be true. Sensitivity and insight are one thing. Truth is another.

This is the point at which we must consider the radical and positive hypothesis put forward by the Roman Catholic Church to the effect that there exists a clearly defined community, brought into being by God through Jesus Christ, to which complete and final authority in matters of interpretation has been given. On this hypothesis the Bible does not stand by itself. The Bible needs the Church as the Church needs the Bible, one complementing the other; but, between the two, a wholly authoritative account of all matters relating to faith and morals can be given to the world in every generation.

The hypothesis can be developed in the following way. From the beginning certain biblical statements have caused confusion. With reference to Paul's letters 2 Pet. 3.16 says, 'There are some things in them hard to understand, which the ignorant and unstable twist to their own destruction, as they do the other scriptures.' It has always been the same. The great disputes of the Church were not between a scriptural party and a non-scriptural party, but between various parties which all supported their arguments by reference to Scripture. In the nineteenth century, when new churches sprang up overnight, especially to the west of the Atlantic, claims were made again and again that now at last the true meaning of Scripture had been revealed. Charles Taze Russell, Joseph Smith, and Mary Baker Eddy were among those who made such assertions.[1] If the Bible is to speak with a single voice, there must be a means of sorting out these claims and declaring unambiguously which are true and· which

[1] Charles Taze Russell, Joseph Smith and Mary Baker Eddy founded the Jehovah's Witnesses, the Church of Jesus Christ of Latter-Day Saints (Mormons) and Christian Science, respectively.

are false. The logic of revelation requires it. It is absurd to suppose that God revealed himself in the flesh, granted to the world a record of his acts in Holy Scripture and then allowed confusion to develop over what the record meant. It must be assumed that God would provide a means of interpretation, independent of the Bible but of equal authority with it, continuous, not static, and infinitely adaptable to circumstances.

The second point in the argument is that such an authority exists—in the Catholic Church. It is maintained that Christ founded an organization with a fixed method of entry, certain definite functions and procedures, and a head and leaders who could teach with undisputed authority. The account of this is to be found in the Gospels, but this does not mean that we have here another of those circular arguments in which the Church vouches for the Gospels and the Gospels vouch for the Church. It is argued that the foundation of the Church by Christ is a historical fact that is established, as are other historical facts, on the basis of contemporary records. In this case the contemporary records happen to be the Gospels, but they are not used in the argument as divine documents at all. They are merely records to be examined and weighed and corroborated if possible. By a strictly historical argument it can be demonstrated that Christ founded a Church which could teach without error. That Church proclaimed the gospel to be the Word of God and everything follows from there.

The third point in the argument introduces us to the word 'tradition'. The word has two senses. It can refer to the *process* whereby ideas and usages are passed on. Folk songs, local customs, children's games, nursery rhymes are preserved by tradition. But the word can also be used for the actual *content* of what is passed on. In theological discussion both senses are common, but we shall speak of the process of tradition when alluding to the former sense and use the word tradition on its own when we mean the content of what is passed on.

According to Catholic teaching the process of tradition began when Jesus instructed the apostles orally in all matters relating to the divine revelation which was summed up in his own person. This instruction was plainly unique. The historical circumstances in which it was given can never be reconstructed and yet it is of universal significance. It was the task of the apostles to convey it in its fullness—and, as the Roman Catholic Church would say, inerrantly—to the next generation and to the world. The task was not easy because one cannot imagine that the original teaching was a neat list of propositions or, indeed, that it was exclusively intellectual; but fulfilment of the task was not dependent on human ingenuity. The process of tradition is guided by the Holy Spirit throughout.

In the course of time the oral message was committed to writing and the apostles died. From this point onwards there are two complementary authorities, the authority of Scripture itself and the authority of the tradition, vested in bishops, to whom, as successors of the apostles, the original teaching was entrusted. Scripture cannot stand by itself. A prior authority was necessary to provide Scripture with its content and to determine the scope of the canon after a number of broadly Christian writings had appeared. And a similar authority was and is necessary to indicate to the faithful which of the many conflicting interpretations of Scripture was the true one. Over against Scripture, which is unchanging, there must be an authority which moves through history, applying the faith to new situations, emphasizing and ensuring continuity of belief, facilitating organic development but rejecting novel and disruptive tendencies. In the Catholic discussion of interpretation Scripture and tradition go hand in hand. The Second Vatican Ecumenical Council (Vatican II) required both to be accepted, 'with equal sentiments and reverence'.[2]

This equality of Scripture and tradition needs emphasis in view of the tendency of critics to assert that Rome exalts tradition over Scripture. Historically tradition came before Scripture. The deposit of faith must have existed before it could be written down. Logically, too, tradition takes precedence in that tradition provided the standards of judgement whereby the Church was able to define the canon. But these arguments are merely formal. No one reading the Dogmatic Constitution on Divine Revelation from Vatican II could reasonably conclude that Scripture was subjugated to tradition. 'Both spring from the same

[2] *Dogmatic Constitution on Divine Revelation* (Catholic Truth Society 1966), p. 11.

77

divine fountain, and so in some manner merge into a unity, and tend towards the same end'.[3]

Scripture belongs with tradition in the Church. It is the Church's task, as it is within her competence alone, to guard and interpret both of them. Roman Catholic theologians speak of the Church's *magisterium*, by which they mean this competence to teach the whole divine truth, as it has been revealed in Christ and embodied in tradition and Scripture, to every generation without error. If this claim is true, it is impossible for anyone outside the Church to criticize the Church on the basis of Scripture, or for anyone inside the Church to criticize the Church along some private and idiosyncratic line. Indeed, the relation of Church to critic is one-sided, for the Church may use Scripture inerrantly against the critic but the critic has no *magisterium* with which to reply. This point was not lost on the early defenders of the faith. Tertullian, the Carthaginian lawyer, a vocal though erratic apologist of the early third century, cut off heresy at the roots by maintaining that all arguments of heretics from Scripture were inadmissible because they lacked the competence to expound Scripture. The Church, on the other hand, possessed the Scriptures *and* the sole right of interpreting them. Her arguments, therefore, were guaranteed in advance.

The Council of Trent formulated decrees on this subject in 1546, and the sense of them has been repeated in tractates and encyclicals on many occasions since. In particular the papal encyclicals *Providentissimus Deus* of 1893, *Spiritus Paraclitus* of 1920 and *Divine Afflante Spiritu* of 1943 bear on the subject, and there is the Dogmatic Constitution on Divine Revelation of Vatican II to which we have already referred. All these sources urge assiduous study of Scripture. The Constitution of Vatican II demands a study of literary forms, cultural attitudes and modes of thought to lay bare, as far as scholarship may, the actual intention of the writer. There is no arid literalism here, nor prejudice, nor presupposition, but rather an urgent desire to discover the original meaning of the text whatever it may have been. Nevertheless there is always the saving clause. 'It is necessary to have a right understanding of the text ... All that has been said about the manner of interpreting

[3] Ibid., p. 11.

78

Scripture is subject ultimately to the Church's judgement; she has the divine commission and the office of preserving and explaining the word of God'.[4]

This combination of rigorous Bible study with dogmatic oversight by the Church can lead to considerable variations in practice. There have been times when the Catholic laity have not been encouraged to show much interest in the Bible on the grounds that unskilled readers can too easily be misled. The truth of the Bible is mediated by the Mass, the devotional manuals, the sermons and instruction of the parish priest. There is no need for the ordinary believer to look much further. This, however, does not represent the stance of the Roman Catholic Church today. As early as 1945 Monsignor Ronald Knox brought out his brilliantly readable translation of the New Testament with full ecclesiastical support, followed by the Old Testament in 1949. Vatican II 'earnestly and expressly' called on the faithful to devote themselves to frequent reading and careful study of Holy Scripture. It was no coincidence that 1966 saw the publication of an English edition of the Jerusalem Bible, which has some claim to being the best English translation of all.

Much of the literary, historical and cultural study of the Bible simply requires great learning in the relevant field, and Vatican II saw the end of that period of insularity in which Catholic authorities viewed non-Catholic biblical learning with suspicion. Today the Catholic student is encouraged to pursue non-dogmatic study of the Bible at the feet of anyone who has a claim to be respected. What the Biblical Commission, set up by Leo XIII in 1902, affirmed about the Synoptic Problem or the authorship of the Pentateuch is no longer the final word. Modern literary criticism has much more to say on these issues, and the Catholic student is given every encouragement to attend to it.

In dogmatic matters, of course, the Church holds fast to its *magisterium*. Critics will say that freedom is permitted only within predetermined limits. Catholics can reply that the hierarchy is simply displaying confidence. Possessing the truth already, it nevertheless promotes exhaustive study of the text and background of the Bible in the assurance that all genuine discovery will confirm the truth. The two elements stand now

[4] Ibid., p. 14f.

as from the beginning: the Bible exhaustively studied and the Church to guide and correct the study and to interpret authentically.

This chapter has not been much concerned with methods of interpretation but rather with presuppositions, for in this particular area the presuppositions are all-important. A further advantage of the Roman Catholic approach is that all methods may be explored. The guarantee of truth does not lie in the method used but in the Church that adjudicates on the findings.

13

THE AUTHORITY OF THE WORD

In the sixteenth century Martin Luther issued a wide-ranging and fundamental challenge to the authority of the Church, and at no point was the challenge more fierce than on the subject of the Bible. There were other challenges to Rome. Indeed the Reformation was made up of so many diverse elements that an exhaustive account of Reformation attitudes to Scripture would be intolerably complicated. It is possible, however, to isolate two strands, two general tendencies that can be traced from the Reformation into the present day. One derives from Luther, the other from John Calvin. These trends will be discussed in this chapter and the next.

Luther was convinced out of his own spiritual experience that the Church enjoyed no absolute competence to interpret the Scriptures without error. His attitude appears to create an immediate problem. Moral and doctrinal issues are constantly raised as the Church passes through history, and Scripture, the unfailing well of Christian truth, does not provide unambiguous answers. How then are the issues resolved?

Many Protestants who stand in succession to Luther claim that to state the question in that way is to pre-judge it. If Scripture is primarily a source of affirmations about faith and morals, some means of distilling those affirmations is necessary. But that is not how Scripture seems to these disciples of the Reformation. To them Scripture is the medium whereby God addresses the believer. It is to be regarded as a living and active word. The result of the encounter between God and the believer is not the definition of dogma but the generation of personal faith. Doctrinal pronouncements are necessary, and they can be drawn from Scripture by the proper exercise of devout scholarship, but Scripture's primary function is to bring God and man face to face. The intervention of an external body, even the Church itself, is intolerable.

It follows that the crucial questions are concerned with the nature of Scripture as a means of revelation. The methods and processes of interpretation will become apparent only when it is clear what Scripture really is.

The first element in this approach is the assertion that God has spoken to mankind fully and finally in Christ. He is the living Word, the perfect expression of all that God is. He has authority that cannot be reproduced by any human agency. Men can bear witness to him. They cannot speak as he speaks. Christ is a *living* Word; that is to say, God chose to reveal himself not through words on a page, but through his Son. Because God chose his Son and that Son is unique, it is not open to any human body to put forward either an institution or a document as an extension of that revelation. The full, perfect and final revelation was through the medium of the flesh. It is seen in Christ, incarnate, crucified, risen and reigning, and in nothing else whatever.

One must, therefore, distinguish carefully between the Word of God in Christ and the words of Holy Scripture. Scripture is not the living Word, even though it consists of irreplaceable documents composed under the guidance of the Holy Spirit and uniquely related to the facts of the revelation in Christ. Christ is the unique revelation. The Bible is unique in that it is the only witness that bears directly on the revelation in Christ. The two kinds of uniqueness are not the same. Christ has authority *in himself*. The Bible has authority through its subject matter and through the facility given to its authors to express that subject matter fully. The Word is infallible, but the biblical words are fallible in that, though they describe infallibility, they are the product, at least in part, of fallible men.

None the less, in the second place, it is contended that Scripture has a dignity that distinguishes it from other literature. While the whole course of history is in God's hand, there is a mid-point, a fulcrum, which is the incarnation. This extends from the birth of Jesus to the death of the last apostolic eyewitness who saw the risen Christ and received his direct commission to bear witness to the world. This is the period of direct revelation and there can be only one such. Those who believed and preached in this period did so from a vantage point that cannot be achieved by any other generation of Christians. The apostles, therefore, had an experience, an authority and a function which no successors could assume. As pre-eminent witnesses they were assisted by inspiration without parallel when they came to write things down. So the Bible emerged. The contribution of the apostles was indispensable, a claim which cannot be made for the writings of any of the bishops, saints and fathers of later times.

From one point of view the New Testament is a human book, but the men who produced it were a small band of apostles of the first generation. Among them the human errors might well be expected to be minimal.

On this hypothesis the formation of the canon was a consequence of the recognition that the apostolic tradition was *sui generis* and incapable of extension. Whatever later developments were necessary, they must be deduced from and controlled by Scripture. The Bible, and particularly the New Testament, is thus regarded as a confessional norm, a standard of Christian affirmation and experience by which all pronouncements of individuals and churches are judged and by which deviations are recognized. It does not matter how far we are carried from the biblical era as the centuries roll by, Scripture remains a permanent witness to the focal event of history and a permanent arbiter to affirm the truth and to exclude the fanciful, the legendary, the erroneous and the corrupt.

Thirdly, because of its nature and function, Scripture needs no other witness to bring it to life. It is wrongly regarded as an ancient text. From the mid-point in time it speaks to the whole of time. It is ever contemporary, for the turning-point of history can never be out of date. Protestants have maintained that, in the Roman Catholic argument, the Bible is regarded as an ancient authority that needs to be constantly interpreted and brought up to date by day-to-day decisions of a living Church. The decisions, too, tend to be dogmatic, leading to a system of beliefs to which the believer must assent. Against this the Protestants affirm that Scripture is a living word to which one must respond with the full commitment of faith. God speaks to the reader of the Bible as person to person, and the response is the same as that of the original hearers of the gospel.

This confidence in the direct and personal nature of the biblical word and its indispensability led to the Reformation doctrine of *sola scriptura*. Scripture stands alone. It is all-sufficient for the believer, all-sufficient for the Church. No one has the right to contradict it, not the Pope, not the fathers, not the councils. It rests on nothing but the Word of God. Augustine had argued, 'I should not believe in the Gospel, did not the Church's authority compel me to do so.'[1] The reformers replied that God verified the gospel and the gospel verified the Church. The place of tradition is thus challenged. Within the apostolic period, it is argued, there is no distinction between Bible and tradition. After the apostolic period, when a separate tradition does appear, it is drawn from and subservient to Scripture. Tradition may codify Scripture, in which case it is authoritative but secondary, or it may add to Scripture, in which case it is unreliable. Battles have raged around such doctrines as the Immaculate Conception and the Bodily Assumption of the Virgin Mary, because they have been based on extra-scriptural data and yet proclaimed as essential elements in revealed truth. For the Protestant nothing can be extra-biblical and essential. It may be extra-biblical and uncertain—this is the position expressed in Article 6 of the Thirty-nine Articles of the Church of England, 'Holy Scripture containeth all things necessary to salvation: so that whatsoever is not read therein, nor may be proved thereby, is not *required* of any man'—or it may be extra-biblical and false; but it cannot be extra-biblical and essential.

Scripture stands alone; but who reads Scripture, and how? The truth of Scripture is not to be received in the same way and on the same level as truth in any other field of knowledge, for the faithful reading of Scripture brings about an encounter between God and man. It is a reciprocal relationship. The Bible inspires faith and faith opens up the Bible. Without faith the Bible is as lifeless as an out-of-date catalogue. Its power is not automatic, operating whether the reader co-operates or not. But if the reader feels as the original writers felt, if his experience coincides in any degree with theirs, if he finds himself sympathetic to their needs and their hopes, the Bible will begin to speak to him and reveal the divine truth. This truth, once grasped, will deepen feeling and extend experience so that,

[1] Augustine's statement can be found in his *Against the Epistle of Manichaeus*, 5.6.

as he reads, the believer will find himself more and more at home. The Bible will speak more and more persuasively and he will have ears to hear. The same words addressed to an unbelieving neighbour would bring forth nothing but a yawn.

The encounter is the work of the Holy Spirit, because he is on both sides of it. Through the Holy Spirit the Bible was composed. Through the Holy Spirit the Bible is read and believed. In this manner the reformers escape from the apparent necessity of an authoritative interpreting body. The external interpreter, no matter how authoritative, cannot penetrate to those sensitive, personal areas where the Spirit works. Through the Spirit the Bible addresses itself to the believer's precise condition. That is, one might say, the miracle of Scripture, for it happens not once or twice, but whenever a humble man takes it up and begins to read.

So far in the discussion of this position we have made no distinction between two different but complementary functions of Scripture. Scripture exists for the believer and is for him a means of communion with God. It also exists for the Church and provides grounds for the Church's teaching. The believer responds by believing and living as a Christian. The Church responds by teaching and preaching. Both responses require faith, but the second demands intellectual and scholarly processes that are not necessary in the first.

If the Bible is the supreme rule of faith and the Church has no separate authority, how does the ecclesiastical scholar formulate Christian teaching, especially in those areas where the Bible is not explicit or is even contradictory? Method will be all-important. Diverse methods are legitimate when there is an arbiter to sift the findings. If there is no arbiter, there must be a simple and direct method of interpretation or the end will be confusion.

Some would say that the Protestant churches provide evidence of precisely that kind of confusion, but this may be due to the fact that modern interpreters have often deserted the rules Luther laid down. To these we turn.

Luther solves the problem of the unity of the Bible by an unqualified claim that the whole Bible is Christian Scripture. Christ is the Lord of the Scriptures and all Scripture preaches Christ. Understanding the Bible means finding Christ in it. This applies as much to the Prophets and the Psalms as to the Gospels. This contention pays scant respect to Judaism as a religion in its own right, but neither medieval Catholicism nor the Reformation churches showed much readiness to take Judaism seriously.

A question arises as to how one is to find Christ in passages that are not remotely relevant to the incarnation. Three things are said in reply. First, God plotted the course of Israel's history towards the final revelation in Christ; all the historical material will, therefore, bear in some way on the final revelation. Second, the apparent irrelevance of many passages may be due to the reader's ignorance. Rigorous exegetical scholarship reveals that much of what appears divergent is part of the main stream. Typological interpretation has a part to play here. Old Testament events that seem to be concerned only with the physical preservation of Israel in fact point forward to the salvation of mankind. Third, when all has been said, Luther accepted the relativity of Scripture. Some books he prized—the Epistles of Paul, the Psalms and the fourth Gospel. Others he showed little sympathy for. His strictures on James and Revelation are notorious, and he did not esteem the Synoptic Gospels as highly as one would expect.

The Christ-principle gives the Bible a focus and simplifies the task of interpretation. It goes some way to counteracting the Roman Catholic claim that Scripture demands an authentic interpreter. If all Scripture is to be related to Christ and find its significance in that relationship, many of the confusions for which an external arbiter is required are resolved.

A second principle enunciated by Luther is that of the perspicuity of Scripture; that is to say, Scripture has a plain, straightforward sense, and that sense and no other provides the true meaning. Scripture is plain enough for every man to understand. No artifice is needed, no scholarly training, simply faith. Literary and historical exegesis extends the meaning, but it is not essential. Scripture can speak for itself. This meant an end to the convoluted interpretations of previous centuries and the fourfold meaning drawn out by medieval scholars. Allegory was allowed to stand only when the biblical author plainly intended it.

By the simple process of reading the Bible in its literal sense, the great themes that surround the incarnation, the holiness of God, the gospel of grace, salvation, the Christian hope, are made known to the humblest reader. Of course obscurities remain.

There is no tidy system, but tidy systems simply satisfy the mind. They do not evoke faith. What does come to light is the inner meaning of Scripture, the heart of the gospel, sufficient for the individual's salvation and for the preaching and teaching of the Church. By this principle of perspicuity the subjective element in interpretation is diminished and the need for an external authority recedes still further.

The third principle is that, when there is serious difficulty, Scripture must be used to interpret Scripture. Even when a passage is set in the context of the full revelation in Christ and read in its plainest sense, it may still cause difficulty. It may appear incomplete or confused or contradictory. In such a case reference must be made not to an external authority, but to other scriptural passages on the same subject. The clear must be allowed to throw light on the less clear. The whole must be allowed to illuminate the particular. From the exegete's point of view the Psalter is among the most problematic books of the Bible, but the spirit of praise and supplication in the Psalter as a whole is unmistakable. The difficult verse must be read in the light of the overall purpose. Similarly the sacrificial passages in Leviticus must be read together with Ps. 51, Rom. 12 and Heb. 10, so that the true biblical notion of sacrifice can appear.

If these three principles are faithfully applied, then, it is claimed, the Word of God will speak to man without need of further interpretation. Christ will address himself to man through the medium of Scripture and the question of authority will become an irrelevance. A man does not believe because he is constrained by authority to accept that certain interpretations are true. He believes because Christ lays hold of him.

It may be objected that, even allowing for the method outlined here, too much is left to the subjectivity of faith. Of this point there can be no final resolution. What to one man is the licence of private judgement to another is the necessary freedom of faith. It may also be objected that disproportionate stress is laid on the first century of the Christian era. Did it all happen then? Is there no comparable continuing revelation? Here we are brought up against the much discussed 'scandal of particularity'. It seems absurd, it may be said, that one decade, one province, one language, one band of villagers should bear the whole weight of the world's redemption. It is absurd, the reply comes; but the foolishness of God is wiser than men. There can, therefore, never be a revelation to compare with Scripture and the lack of proportion will remain always.

Many Protestants argue that, though seeing the Bible in this way does not resolve all theological arguments, it does make the Bible come alive. The common man, the miller's maid, the boy of nine, as Luther said, can know as much about divine truth as the Pope himself. That was the purpose of the incarnation and therein lies the liberty of the Christian man.

14

THE AUTHORITY OF THE TEXT

There are many Protestants who have considerable sympathy with the position outlined in the last chapter but who judge that it has certain notable weaknesses. These critics are variously described as fundamentalists, literalists, believers in plenary or verbal inspiration, or conservative evangelicals. All these terms mean different things, but for the moment it will be useful if we think of a single group of interpreters who reject the kind of Protestant orthodoxy we have just described because it pays insufficient regard to the divine character of the whole Bible and allows for discrimination within the Scriptures. Just as the thesis of the last chapter was argued from Luther, so this more rigorous approach is often traced back to Calvin. Broadly speaking this is just, but it must not be supposed that Luther and Calvin were at odds in their fidelity to the Scriptures, still less that Luther was ambivalent or broad-minded on the subject. Both men faced Rome and the centuries of ecclesiastical tradition with the Bible as their only defence. In the succeeding century Luther's followers were scarcely less rigorous than Calvin's. None the less it is reasonable to see in the work of John Calvin the starting-point of a doctrine of Holy Scripture that is clearly distinguishable from that of the last chapter.

The difference between the two men and the two approaches has something to do with temperament. Luther was the passionate, lion-hearted prophet, the man of deep, soul-searching experiences, who did not shrink from making his own judgements because nothing was more real or more authentic to him than the inward witness of the Spirit confirming the message of Scripture. Calvin was the logician, the lawyer, the organizer, at once more cool and more persistent in following arguments to their logical end. Calvin could not rest until he had built up a comprehensive doctrinal system on the basis of Scripture, and he revised it again and again in pursuit of completeness and clarity. The first edition of the *Institutes of the Christian Religion* was published in 1536 as a relatively brief theological handbook for French Protestants. The final edition of 1559 consisted of four books and seventy-nine chapters. The *Institutes* are renowned for their logic and precision. With meticulous care Calvin pursued every scriptural idea and worked it into his system. Nothing was too obscure or too intractable. Calvin is best known for his unsentimental approach to the doctrine of predestination, and that issue reveals the remorseless logic that drove him on. To Calvin human sensibility was irrelevant. What logic drew from Scripture was true. The will and pleasure of men are not to be set against the word of the Holy Spirit.

Calvin differed from Luther in his estimation of the actual words of Scripture. Luther revered the words because they were the medium by which the Word was known. Calvin held that the whole Bible came from God and that every word had its place in the divine economy. He did not allow himself to pass over passages on the pretext that no christocentric element could be found in them. What God had given in Scripture was not to be brought to the bar of human judgement. It was to be believed and obeyed.

The first stages in the argument are simple and familiar. If God has acted in Christ, there must be some means whereby the facts of the incarnation and their meaning can be made known to people in every time and place. However significant the encounter with the risen Christ is, it is impossible until some basic knowledge of the life, death and resurrection of Jesus has been gained. No missionary ever burst in on an unevangelized tribe to discover that they had encountered the risen Christ already. The Christ event has to be translated into words that witness both to the fact and to the meaning before it can be effective. On this all Christians agree. Literalists go one step further. They hold that the words must be authenticated by God himself to remove for ever the possibility of confusion and wishful thinking in this most vital area. They put their faith in the text. Scripture, in its entirety, is the Word of God, and neither man nor Church has any right to add to, subtract from, vary or dispute its contents in any way whatever.

This, of course, is an argument from a Christian context. Something similar could be said about other sacred writings and, indeed, is said by Muslims about the Qur'an. A similar argument is current in Judaism. It is not enough to say that God acted in Israel's history. He also gave the Word, the Torah, so that the Exodus event might endure for ever, and all faithful Jews walk in the freedom and the discipline which first came to Israel through that event. Literalism is possible wherever there is a sacred text.

In a sense Christian literalists pay reverence to a double authority, Christ and Scripture, and they are happy to see them as complementary and analogous. To the objection that each passage of Scripture is written in a human language and suffers the limitations of vocabulary and syntax of that language, to say nothing of the cultural limitations imposed by the setting in a deprived and isolated country in the ancient Near East, the literalist replies that precisely the same restrictions apply to the incarnation itself. The Son of God was a man of one tongue, little education, and Hebrew culture. God willed it so. It might be considered reasonable to object to Christianity altogether on these grounds, but it is not reasonable to accept a small-town carpenter as Saviour of the world and to object to the notion of an infallible record on the grounds that it has a limited vocabulary. Something similar can be said on the question of inerrancy. If one can accept that God became man and lived as man without sin, there is no problem in the contention that God spoke through his servants, the prophets and evangelists, without error.

The word 'literalist' needs further clarification. It is obvious that the text of the Bible has suffered all the normal misfortunes of transmission; pages have been damaged and lost, copyists have grown tired and made mistakes, translators have nodded, and so on. Scholars have done their best to remedy these misfortunes, and there is no need to doubt that a good modern translation represents not only substantially, but also in detail, the same body of affirmations as the original documents long since lost. None the less, errors have crept in and, where absolute authority is under discussion, there is no room for error at all. The argument of the literalist is that, for every Bible book, there was an original pure and authentic text, given by God through the medium of human writers, but given without error.

That text is literally accurate in that it states in every detail what God wished to say. Our Bibles depart a little from these originals but, in the providence of God, they do not depart very much. As far as meaning goes, they are reliable, but they do not have the same literal accuracy as the originals. Literalism is thus both a good and a bad name for this approach. It is good in that it suggests acceptance of the whole Bible, without any modifications whatever, as the authentic Word of God to man. It is bad in that it suggests a slavish adherence to the lettter even in translation and even when the sense is lost. The true literalist allows that there may be minor confusions in an English version and devotes himself to the study of the text to see if those confusions can be removed. He is convinced that the nearer he can get to the original, the less confusion there will be, for with God words and meaning exactly coincide.

Something now needs to be said about two terms, 'conservative evangelical' and 'fundamentalist', which give rise to misunderstanding. Neither is entirely precise. The word 'evangelical' refers to a general approach to the Christian faith in which stress is laid on the atoning death of Jesus, salvation by faith and personal conversion. Evangelicals tend towards literalism, but there are many who would be as much at home in the previous chapter as in this one. The word 'conservative' suggests two things: first the desire to conserve the Christian faith as it has always been, and second, an unwillingness to accept critical arguments about the provenance of biblical books before they have been proved up to the hilt. For example, there is considerable support among biblical scholars for the propositions that the book of Isaiah had many authors living in different times and places, that Daniel was not written until about 165 B.C., that 2 Peter did not come from the pen of the apostle, and so on. Conservatives are not easily persuaded on matters like these.

Similarly in the matter of history they do not easily give way to scepticism. Critics have argued that, because the sun cannot stand still, Josh. 10.12–14 is in error, and because waters will not pile up in a heap, Exod. 14.22, 29 is in error, and so on. Conservatives are disinclined to accept such reasoning. They argue that God is not subject to his own laws, that he is able to do any of the things that Scripture describes and that, if his Word clearly states that something happened, one must accept that it did. It is possible to be more or less conservative in matters like these. Some conservatives will listen to no critical arguments at all; others are ready to agree with conclusions that have been cogently argued and do not conflict with their theological presuppositions.

'Fundamentalism' is a term commonly used to describe the conservative, literalist approach, but it originally referred to a movement in the U.S.A. in the early 1900s. The fundamentalists believed that there was not merely wholesale profanity outside the Church but fatal apostasy within it. They set themselves vigorously to affirm the basic elements or fundamentals of Christianity, and these included the inerrancy of the Bible. Unfortunately terms like 'fundamentalist' and its supposed opposite, 'modernist', have been degraded in theological polemic so that it is not easy to use them without some kind of overtone. It is hoped that here emotional and judgemental overtones have been avoided and the terms used in their proper sense alone.

The fundamentalist-literalist argues that he is not an innovator. His approach is drawn from the Bible itself and from the words of Jesus. Sacred Scripture already existed in New Testament times. Jews and Christians alike accepted the Jewish Scriptures as the Word of God and did not question their accuracy. Paul did not question the existence of Adam and Abraham, nor did he throw doubt on the facts of the Exodus and the wanderings in the wilderness. Jesus himself, while frequently at odds with those who added to the Scriptures, accepted the authenticity of the Scriptures themselves. The New Testament takes Old Testament history for granted. It assumes that the events recounted took place in the manner described. Christian apologetic in the New Testament is based upon the soundness of prophecy. It was argued that Jesus was Messiah because the words of the prophets pointed forward to him. Several times at the beginning of Matthew's Gospel the formula, 'that it might be fulfilled which was spoken by the prophet', or something like it, links a prophecy with a statement about Jesus. The same is true of the speeches in the early chapters of Acts.

New Testament writers build up their doctrine by citation from the Old Testament and validate their teaching by showing that it was based upon the Old Testament Scriptures. When Paul, in Rom. 3, wishes to prove that all men are sinful, he produces a catena of quotations from Psalms, Proverbs and Isaiah which is sufficient for his argument. If further proof is needed it is provided by Deut. 4.2 and Rev. 22.18f. Both texts affirm that the matter in the books concerned is final and unalterable. Nothing must be added and nothing taken away.

Jews and Christians were, and still are, able to take this view because of their understanding of inspiration. Given theistic propositions, a reasonable case can be put forward for special revelation in the text of Scripture. It is often asserted that a *man* may be inspired by God but his *writing*, or whatever other activity he is concerned with, will still show marks of human fallibility. The literalist replies that this is not what Scripture says. 2 Tim. 3.16 asserts that the writing itself is inspired and is effective because of that inspiration. When one looks more closely it appears that inspiration relates to the origin of the writing, not to its present condition or status or function. The reason why Scripture is profitable is that it came into being under conditions of inspiration and, having been so inspired, it will always be true.

Inspiration in this sense means that God determined the content, character and meaning of the writing and that man was the means whereby it was set down and promulgated. This is how the prophets speak of themselves. 'Men spake from God, being moved by the Holy Ghost', so that it is the word of prophecy to which we must take heed, not the prophet himself (2 Pet. 1.19–21). The prophet begins his oracle with, 'Thus saith the Lord'. The Lord God speaks and the prophet can do nothing but prophesy, that is to say, allow himself to be taken up into the purpose of God (Amos 3.8). The principle accepted by the New Testament writers is illustrated in John 11.50f., where a profound prophetic statement is put on the lips of the treacherous Caiaphas. This is not normal but it is possible, and it shows that the word can be inspired when the speaker is not. This brings us to verbal and plenary inspiration. In the particular instance when God wishes to create Scripture, he puts his words into human mouths and human minds. What is written in the original Scripture is, therefore, word by word, fully inspired, and questions of relative truth do not arise.

This contention gives rise to the objection that the process is mechanical, that human beings are reduced to automata. The harshness of these metaphors really obscures the point. Men, who are accustomed to talk volubly, are taken up into the purpose of God. God does not destroy their natural faculties and make them speak or write a language that is foreign to them. Amos, under inspiration, does not talk like Plato nor Paul like Apollos. God has infused his divine truth into their natural language. In style these inspired passages are not different from the rest of their speech, but in essence they are different. Paul, disputing with a captain on the cost of a passage, would no doubt reveal the same vigour and passion as we see in Galatians, but the record of such a dispute would be of no consequence to us if we possessed it; that dispute would reveal the man Paul, whereas Galatians, stylistically the same, reveals the Word of God.

It is easy to see now why a literalist view of Scripture goes hand in hand with a conservative view on literary criticism. Linking this process of inspiration with modern notions of literary transmission is not impossible, but it does complicate the picture. The Word of God could be established by the long process of transmission and editing over the years, but it seems wasteful and unnecessary. Consequently, those who take the view that God speaks his own words precisely in Scripture are inclined to accept simpler explanations of the provenance of Bible books, especially where the books claim a single authorship.

If this account of inspiration is true, it follows that the words of the Bible are wholly reliable and trustworthy. There is no need to doubt them in any way whatever, and there is no need for any outside control of them. Simple faith and reverence alone are needed. The problem is not how to answer hypothetical questions from literary critics, nor how to harmonize the teaching of the Bible with modern thought, whatever that may be, but to discern the ways of God and believe and act upon them.

There is, of course, one unavoidable literary issue; that is the difference between the two Testaments. This is usually settled by reference to different dispensations in the history of grace. It was God's will in Old Testament times to reveal some things in part or in figure, and it is inevitable that, after the full revelation in Jesus, the partial character of the old should be manifest.

The Old Testament is not false but incomplete. The process is not one of contradiction but of fulfilment.

On the basis of this understanding of the Bible it is possible to build up a complete theology and rule of life. Its strength lies in its simplicity. Compromising views of the Bible lead to the question, 'If you can doubt one statement, how can you put your trust in any other?' Or, to put it another way, 'If you are prepared to heed the scriptural doctrine of God, of man, of Christ, why not the scriptural doctrine of Scripture?'

None the less the affirmation of the inerrancy of Scripture is constantly challenged. The literalist answers that it is not so much a matter of logic as of attitude. Scripture is not a rag-bag that we have to sort out to find something of value. It is a word requiring unquestioning acceptance and surrender. Not, he would say, that the difficulties are great. Many of them are the product of over-zealous imagination. Many can be sorted out by faithful scholarship. Some must be left as part of the unfathomable mystery of revelation. Furthermore, the Word of God proves itself again and again as it is fulfilled in history and confirmed in experience.

It is true that the basis of the literalist's position is the Bible's witness to itself, but he is not without an answer when charged with arguing in a circle. Self-witness is not necessarily false. It may be the truest witness of all, and in the case of God's self-witness it must be so. Again, external, supporting argument, however desirable, is not possible in such a case as this. There is no way of bringing evidence to prove or disprove empirically that God spoke here and there. To put it another way, supreme authority must be self-authenticating, and one must approach it not with logic but with faith. As Calvin says, 'Let it be considered, then, as an undeniable truth that they who have been inwardly taught of the Spirit feel an entire acquiescence in the Scripture, and that it is self-authenticated, carrying with it its own evidence, and ought not to be made the subject of demonstration and arguments from reason; but that it obtains the credit which it deserves with us by the testimony of the Spirit.'[1]

All this adds up to the assertion of the intrinsic nature of the Bible's authority. The position calls for an attitude of great

[1] Calvin, *Institutes*, 1.7.5. This can be found in J. T. McNeill, ed., *The Library of Christian Classics*, vol. 20 (S.C.M. Press 1961), p. 80.

humility, great patience and great faith, because difficulties such as those outlined in Part 1 recur constantly. None the less it is widespread among devout people.

15

THE LIBERAL APPROACH

Unfortunately the term 'liberal', more than any term used in this book, lacks clear definition. There is political, moral and theological liberalism. In theological usage there are liberal Jews, liberal Catholics, liberal Protestants and liberal Evangelicals. There are many who are liberal in some respects and not in others. It is possible to be more or less liberal, as it is possible to be more or less conservative. The liberal movement was by no means homogeneous, the British version being significantly different from the Continental one.

The genesis of the movement is to be found in a new mood that settled on Europe in the early years of the last century. Rationalism, the contention that traditional structures of belief and behaviour should be submitted to the harsh tests of human logic and not defended by appeals to the supernatural, had begun to undermine the pillars of authority everywhere. Romanticism, a movement far removed in spirit from rationalism, continued the process, for the romantics pursued the cult of personal feeling and had no love for the monumental and impersonal authority of institutions.

At this point F. E. D. Schleiermacher (1768-1834) came on the scene. Few names are more important in the history of European religious thought. Deeply concerned about religion, he began not with revelation or reason, but with religious experience. Religion for him was not orthodoxy, ecclesiastical or rational, but a sense and taste for the infinite, an awareness of absolute dependence. After Schleiermacher the way was open for an interpretation of the Christian faith that left man free to make his own discoveries and to affirm his own beliefs.

Three different notions of religious authority were thus in circulation. First there was the ecclesiastical, the notion that authority was based on revelation, guaranteed by tradition, preserved in a divine institution and often supported by the state; as such it could be imposed on the individual, whose responsibility was to submit and subscribe to whatever formularies the institution defined. Second there was the rational, the notion that authority derived from the rigorous exercise of reason, which may or may not have been regarded as a divine gift; whatever had the support of reason was true, whether it conformed to tradition or not, and no man and no institution had the right to resist what was thus publicly demonstrated. Third there was the personal, the notion that a man's inner sensibility was of greatest importance; whatever part institution and reason played, they should not overrule conscience, which was the supreme arbiter and final authority in any individual's religion.

These three notions can be combined in various ways. This accounts for the many different versions of liberalism. On the continent of Europe a liberal Protestant theology developed which, in its extreme form, came near to transforming Christian faith into a diffuse, Christ-orientated humanism. Let us consider how one or two central doctrines were treated.

All Christians agree that there is a general revelation of God in the created universe, but most would say that it is incomplete. The perfect revelation came at a particular place and a particular time. Liberal Protestants distrusted the notion of special revelation because, on one hand, it suggested an interruption of the normal working of the universe and, on the other, it appeared unfair. Certain people—presumably those near the event—would have an advantage, which seemed to imply a flaw in God's love for all mankind. Liberal Protestants were therefore inclined to stress general revelation and to reduce the particularity of the incarnation to the minimum. They emphasized the humanity of Jesus and laid less stress on his divine nature and his miraculous powers. That in turn led to a largely moral view of salvation. Liberals did not readily speak, as Evangelicals did, of the once-for-all nature of the sacrifice of Christ on Calvary. Rather they thought of the death of Christ as a sublime example of human courage and fidelity. The church was conceived of not as an authoritative institution, but as a company of like-minded people drawn together by common sympathy and ideals. The significant factor was not the divine nature of the community itself but the moral appeal that drew the members together. One of the most important books to emerge from the centre of the liberal movement on the Continent was Adolf Harnack's *What is Christianity?*, a verbatim record of sixteen lectures given in Berlin in the winter of 1899-1900. Two quotations will suffice. Both expound Protestantism as Harnack understood it. On authority: 'It [Protestantism] protested against all formal, external authority in religion; against the authority, therefore, of councils, priests, and the whole tradition of the Church. That alone is to be authority which shows itself to be such within and effects a deliverance.'[1] On the gospel and the Church: 'Protestantism reckons upon the Gospel being something so simple, so divine, and therefore so truly human, as to be most certain of being understood when it is left entirely free, and also as to produce essentially the same experiences and convictions in individual souls.'[2]

In Britain the movement was less diverse than on the Continent. There was no iconoclastic wing, but there was a sober, erudite tradition of liberal critical scholarship to which the modern Church is still in debt. Though not anti-authoritarian on principle, British liberals did scrutinize the old standards. New ideas were abroad. The scale of human vision had been enlarged dramatically by scientists and explorers. The liberals were anxious that the Christian faith should move with the times and not cling to forms of authority which had operated successfully in the past but had no place in the future. It was no longer sufficient to say, 'The Bible says ...', 'The Church teaches ...'. It must also be shown that the affirmations of Bible and Church commended themselves to the mind and conscience of the believer. Reason and feeling provided proper tests for Christian statements. In this respect the Church had nothing to fear. Its gospel, simply stated, was readily commendable. If some of the more abstruse tenets suffered, that was a proper price to pay for keeping Christian theology in touch with the times. Sometimes the accommodation of Christian belief to the spirit of the age was positive and beneficial. For example, the general belief in progress enabled liberal theologians to give a new dimension to Christian hope. Worshippers in Queen Victoria's day could sing, 'These

[1] Adolf Harnack, *What is Christianity?*, 3rd English ed. (1904), p. 282.
[2] Ibid., p. 279.

things shall be', and think of it not as an apocalyptic vision, but as a practical programme.

How does this relate to the interpretation of the Bible? In the first place it was a liberal principle that the Bible stood by its own intrinsic quality and not by virtue of supernatural origin. Most interpreters assume that the Bible is different in kind from other literature, not because of any empirical difference, but because of a unique quality deriving from its divine provenance. Liberals are hesitant about notions of uniqueness and more interested in whatever empirical differences there may be. They argue that the great inspiring Spirit is at work in all times and places and bringing to birth, in all societies, great literature of every kind. There is no essential discontinuity between literature and Bible. Experience may show that the Bible is supreme in the literature known to western man, but it is not unique *a priori*. It is supreme because it speaks more frequently and more profoundly to the human condition than any other book.

The reason for the intrinsic quality of the Bible can be expressed in two ways. Humanly speaking it gained its quality from the sifting process of the centuries. In two millennia almost everything happened to Israel. Hardly an experience that could lift or shatter the human soul was missed, and every kind of literary response was made. The corporate memory preserved only the best. Where else in the world does such a lore exist? It is not surprising that, in our culture, the Bible appears unique. Theologically speaking, the whole process belongs to the purpose of God. He guided Israel, raised up prophets and inspired psalmists to record their visions and express their thoughts. In the providence of God, Israel's experience of those days of agony and ecstasy has become the inspiration of the whole world.

The virtue of the Bible, therefore, lies in the fact that it is a treasury of human experience, a moving record of a nation's struggle for faith. It is capable of illuminating so many different situations. Across the continents and the centuries it can stir and enrich men of all kinds. It reaches its climax in the story of the purest love this world has ever seen. From the liberal point of view, that is the essence of the claim that it is the Word of God.

Secondly and consequently, the liberal interpreter is inclined to be wary of the miraculous element in the Bible. To say that

Jesus is sublime in nature is one thing; to say that he is supreme over nature is quite another. A Jesus who could turn water into wine would not be the same sympathetic figure as the one who loved and suffered as other men do. If Jesus is to be imitated, and the imitation of Jesus was the heart of the matter for liberals, the miracle stories can be obstacles. Some are admirable as demonstrations of compassion, but as historical incidents they do not help, for the miraculous is, by definition, the exceptional, and as such it provides little encouragement for those who live in a world where the exceptional does not happen.

Liberals therefore tend to question the historical accuracy of the miracle stories, though it should also be said that their espousal of diligent, critical methods would have led to this end, whether it suited their Christology or not. Some miracle stories are regarded as exaggerations. Jairus' daughter was not dead but asleep (Mark 5.35–43 and parallels). Others are better understood as psychosomatic cures which, due to the ignorance of the day, were thought to be miracles. The man at the pool of Bethesda did not *want* to be cured until he met Jesus, who gave him a new desire to live (John 5.1–15). Others may be natural happenings which have been inaccurately reported. The feeding of the five thousand might be explained by the fact that the boy, standing forward and giving all he had, moved the others to bring out rations which they were selfishly keeping back (John 6.1–14). Others might be the result of pious imagination. The wonder story was an accepted method of rendering honour to a celebrated figure.

The cause of this diminution of the miraculous was not scepticism but a devout, liberal faith. The incarnation reveals the true and living way. It is a difficult way, but not impossible for the common man to walk in. Jesus may have been unique in his fidelity to God's purpose, but fidelity to God's purpose is not beyond the competence of ordinary men of good will.

This means, thirdly, that the liberal interpretation of Scripture is more concerned with questions about what Jesus actually said and did than with doctrinal affirmations about his true nature. Liberal critics tried to tease apart elements of the New Testament that deal with the historical facts about Jesus and those that reveal the early Church affirming its faith by applying to him exalted titles that derive from the Old Testament

The former are valuable as they provide Christians with a good practical guide; the latter are transient concepts, significant in the first century but without much meaning in modern times.

One aspect of liberal scholarship can be seen in what is known as 'the quest of the historical Jesus'. The assumption of the quest was that the story of the real Jesus of Nazareth, as it was known to the earliest Christians, was subsequently distorted by Christian apologists who were anxious to find a way of commending the faith to the Roman world. The empire would not be impressed by the appeal of a humble Jewish carpenter. If Roman lives were to be turned upside down—Christianity meant that in the first century—stronger arguments would be needed. If Roman pride and glory were to yield to Christian faith and love, a categorical authority would be called for. The Christian apologists, therefore, represented Jesus of Nazareth as the supreme Lord, the divine Son, the mystical Saviour. In this language the New Testament was written. In modern times the task of scholars is to set on one side the Christ who was the construct of the apologists and rediscover Jesus of Nazareth. The liberal critics argue that the apologists were successful but misleading. Honorific titles clouded the issue. The humble teacher *was* the divine Word. Many lives of Jesus were written to prove this point. They tried to avoid dogmatic theory and present to the modern world a Jesus who was firmly grounded in history, who revealed God's ways to men, and who could serve as an inspiration to modern Christians.

Together with the quest went research into the teaching of Jesus. It was assumed that the supreme teacher of the human race had provided, besides his perfect example, a verbal account of the true life. It would not be found in precise teaching that belonged to a particular context but in moral principles that could be acted upon anywhere. Much of the New Testament qualifies, particularly some of the parables and the Sermon on the Mount, but other parts did not yield so easily to this treatment; so, for example, Paul's arguments about original sin and the need of man for the perfect act of expiation were neglected. This meant that the New Testament, and even more the Old Testament, was read selectively. The liberals did not entertain the view that the Bible was equally inspired throughout.

Fourthly, the contemporary belief in progress was employed to explain some of the troublesome notions that appear in the Bible. The harsh laws, the bloodthirsty commands, the ceremonial niceties, the polygamy, the preoccupation with blood sacrifice which occur in the Old Testament were regarded as indications that man, at that stage, still had marks of the primitive about him. The redeeming process, whereby man was slowly liberated from the base nature of the beast was, however, at work. The prophets illustrate the progress, none more so than the unknown author of Isa. 40–55 who gave us the matchless portrait of the Suffering Servant. By New Testament times all the crudities had disappeared and the revelation of the true life was made plain in Jesus.

The same kind of argument was used to sort out the contradictions in the New Testament account of the Kingdom of God. There are passages which present it as a supernatural event to be unfolded by God when the Son of Man returns on clouds of glory at the last day. The details can be traced back to Jewish apocalyptic. This is a version of the Kingdom of God that has little meaning outside the context of first-century Judaism. Its talk of catastrophic finales does not accord with the way that history has unfolded. There are, however, other passages which speak about the Kingdom as a present reality, a realm of truth and love, which grows and grows till it embraces all mankind. This does accord with the facts, particularly, let it be remembered, the facts of Europe in the period before 1914. Civilization was expanding, man was becoming ever more confident, and it seemed reasonable to suppose that the realm of truth and love would be achieved in time. So again the New Testament was read selectively, one parable was taken and another left, and the kingdom was defined not in apocalyptic terms, but as 'the organization of humanity by action inspired by love'.[3]

What is outlined in this chapter is not so much a method of interpretation as an approach or an attitude. The search is not for affirmations that have to be believed but for qualities that inspire and examples that can be followed. Different people read Scripture on different occasions, all seeking guidance for their own situations. Each encounters truth, but each must apply

[3] The definition derives from the work of a famous German liberal theologian, Albrecht Ritschl (1882-9).

it in his own way. Man is not thus demeaned, as he is when a system of belief is imposed upon him. He is rather exposed to perfection and then given the responsibility of living it out for himself. That is true freedom. It makes the formulation of doctrine difficult, but it also makes heresy trials impossible. It raises problems about who is a Christian and who is not, but it obviates schism and strife.

The liberal approach has suffered attacks, particularly from Karl Barth and his followers, but Harnack's question still has to be answered. What is Christianity? Is it an authoritative system that compels belief, or is it, as the liberal believes, a divine influence in the world, incarnated in Jesus, and inspiring men of all kinds to live godly lives? Because the latter will always be an important element in Christian faith, liberal values will never disappear completely from Christian discourse. The liberals do not constitute a school in the present theological world, and few modern interpreters describe themselves as out and out liberals, but liberal attitudes and liberal values appear, in greater or less degree, in the work of most of them.

16

EXISTENTIALISM

One notable feature of the liberal approach was the shift in balance from the source of biblical truth to the audience for whom it was interpreted. In chapters 12, 13 and 14 we considered the arguments of those who were greatly concerned with the authority of the Word of God and not so much concerned with its credibility. The liberals had doubts about this stance. They could not expect their contemporaries to believe some of the statements of the Bible, so they began to throw doubt on the statements, and they were ultimately criticized for allowing nineteenth-century ideals to determine what the Bible had to say, rather than the other way round.

Now, in the last few decades, has come a more radical attack on the credibility of the Bible. It is linked with that form of philosophical understanding known as existentialism, and, though it has appeared in different forms in both Judaism and Catholicism, it is best known from the work of its Lutheran advocate, Rudolf Bultmann. The radical nature of the attack cannot be denied, but this is no reason to judge it hastily. Bultmann's plea is that he is trying to make the Bible significant for modern man and, as we shall see, there are ways in which, as a good Lutheran, he contends for orthodox positions that the liberals had undermined.

Bultmann is concerned with what he calls the mythology of the Bible, and it is well to begin with the understanding of this word. Mythology is sometimes supposed to refer to stories which are untrue and therefore of no consequence or, alternatively, to stories which are untrue and therefore downright mischievous. On these grounds, to speak about mythology in the New Testament, as Bultmann does, is for some devout believers irreverent and offensive. To argue in this way, however, is to use the word 'mythology' inexactly and to do Bultmann a serious injustice.

Few people suppose nowadays that the purpose of myths in pre-literary societies was to give as correct an account as possible of the nature of the universe. Anthropologists have now had ample opportunity of studying the myths of the Greeks, the Egyptians, the Chinese, the American Indians and others, and have reached the conclusion that a more interesting process is taking place than guessing how things might have begun, how the universe was constructed and how it might end. The process begins with man reflecting upon the conditions of his life, on the contradictions that exist in the natural order, in society and in himself. He struggles to explain his experiences, but cannot do so in terms of his own physical being and the visible and tangible world. So he conceives of agencies and realities over and beyond the seen and the tangible that help to determine his existence. Words like 'agency' and 'reality' trip lightly off the tongues of those who discuss these matters in a sophisticated modern language, but our forefathers had simpler literary tools. They could describe the unseen only as if it were essentially the same as the seen. Consequently they thought not of forces and realities but of gods and demons, and they set them in a world entirely like their own. The mythology, therefore, has to be read not as a pre-scientific statement of how things are, but as a symbolic account in narrative form of all the hopes and fears and tensions and frustrations of personal and communal life. Myth is the literary consequence, sometimes profound and often moving, of man's restless endeavours to understand and come to terms with his own existence.

Certain features of mythology are universal. All human life is concerned with love and war, birth and death, summer and winter, day and night, and so there are certain constant factors in mythology. In other ways human experience varies widely. Some men live in the desert and feel the long, hot summer to be the harbinger of death. Others live in northern lands and dread the wet, cold winter. It follows that the actual mythological worlds constructed by different peoples in different places will differ considerably, although they are concerned with the same basic experiences. Those who hunt the bison will have a different notion of how the dead occupy themselves from those who till the soil or live by fishing.

107

It is clear then that the least satisfactory way of weighing a particular mythology is to ask whether it correctly represents what we know from scientific discovery to be true of the physical universe. The most constructive way is to ask how sensitively it expresses, for those who use it, the whole truth about the human condition.

This discussion of mythology has been necessary because the existentialist approach to biblical interpretation, which is linked with the name of Bultmann, begins precisely at this point. It is contended that the New Testament is full of mythology, that the most exalted affirmations of the Christian faith are set out in mythological form.

Let us begin with cosmology—the account of how the universe is constructed to shelter both seen and unseen beings. Every mythology involves a cosmology. Gods and men, the living and the dead, all must have a home somewhere. The Jews had their cosmology and the New Testament takes it over.[1] It has three tiers. In the middle is the earth where man is. Above are the heavens where God is, and below is Sheol where the dead are. So Jesus descended at his death to Sheol, but after three days he broke open the gates, returned to earth and subsequently ascended into heaven.

God, men and the dead, however, are not the only inhabitants of the universe. Tragic accidents, unexpected illness, bitter experience of frustration and perhaps the fact of mortality led the Jews to affirm that the universe was a battleground in which God contended against a multitude of inferior cosmic powers. It was not given to man to understand precisely how the war was going, but from time to time he could see in his affairs evidence of an onslaught from one side or the other. God and the spirits of evil did not contend in the open, but secretly and invisibly. Thus any notable advance one way or the other came unexpectedly. A serious illness meant a demonic attack. A cure was a divine triumph. Both were miraculous, but miracles were taken for granted. The notion of a battle suggests a final victory, and

[1] See, for example, C. M. Jones, ed., *Old Testament Illustrations* (Cambridge University Press 1971), pp. 26f., where three ancient cosmologies appear side by side. The matter is carried much further by C. Blacker and M. Loewe, *Ancient Cosmologies*. Allen and Unwin 1975.

the mythology of the period is full of details of the ultimate encounter when the demons strive to reduce the universe to chaos and God, in the last struggle, overcomes them and brings them to judgement.

All this is very colourful and, some would say, not very edifying, but Bultmann contends that the New Testament presupposes this background. He does not say that, here and there, New Testament writers were reduced to borrowing the odd idea from Jewish apocalyptic and Gnostic myths, but that the New Testament is written throughout in this idiom. That is not a criticism of the New Testament. It is one of the inescapable facts of literature that it must use the cultural tools available. Had anyone existed *per impossibile* who could have spoken in non-mythological language, the common people would not have understood what he was talking about. This reveals one important difference between Bultmann and the liberals. The liberals were embarrassed by what they tended to look upon as biblical naiveties, and they tried to minimize the importance of mythology, to concentrate on the passages where mythology was subdued. Bultmann will have none of this. For him the New Testament must be unravelled as it stands. No picking and choosing is possible because mythology is everywhere. To imagine otherwise is to retreat from the evidence and live in a world of refined but non-biblical modernity.

The approach we are dealing with here claims to be thoroughly positive. As a Lutheran, Bultmann was anxious to let the New Testament speak. To him it was the lively word of God; but the mythology had to be cracked, like the shell of a nut, to reveal the kernel. Truth is not in the mythology, but in the New Testament understanding of human existence. The problem for the interpreter is to grasp that understanding apart from the means of expression. So Bultmann proceeds to the process known as demythologizing.

It might be objected at this point that the mythology so called is all part of the biblical message and that it must be accepted as part of the divine revelation. Not all mythologies are on the same level. The Greeks, the Sumerians, the Egyptians constructed their universes, but they were merely constructions. The Jews constructed theirs under divine inspiration and it is authentic. God chose a place and a time and a language and a culture for his final revelation and he chose a 'mythology' too. So this 'mythology' is particular, revelatory and unique. It corresponds to reality in a way that other mythologies do not.

In reply Bultmann makes three points. First, one cannot accept a mythology at will. If, because of one's birth and environment, one does not accept the New Testament cosmology, there is nothing one can do about it. The New Testament propounds a faith for the world. If that faith is dependent upon its followers achieving an impossible mental feat, it is an absurdity. Second, there is nothing specifically Christian about Jewish mythology. It is not virtuous to believe it nor villainous to deny it. Even supposing one could bring one's mind to do the impossible, it would not represent an advance in Christian understanding. Third, the notion that faith depends upon this kind of intellectual activity is a denial of the New Testament gospel. It makes salvation dependent on mental achievement. So the believer must demythologize the New Testament, that is to say, find his way to the affirmations about existence that lie at its heart and believe as the New Testament writers believed but without their views of the universe. So out go the cosmology, the three-tier universe, the descending and ascending, the unnatural miracles, the notion of rites that work with instrumental efficacy. What remains is the challenge of New Testament faith, to trust God where one is and as one is with one's whole being.

Such a programme, Bultmann affirms, is not untrue to the New Testament but rather follows out the New Testament's own logic. The New Testament does not propose a prescriptive mythology but rather introduces several contradictory mythologies. It begins the process of demythologizing itself. The fourth Gospel differs from the Synoptics for, being composed several decades later, it arises from a situation in which Jewish apocalyptic was already beginning to outgrow its usefulness. The great judgement at the last day which is to be found, for example, in Matt. 25 is replaced in John by the judgement that is already operating within the world (John 3.19; 12.31). The resurrection to the sound of trumpets that Paul describes in 1 Cor. 15 becomes the eternal life that is known already to the faithful (John 17.3; 11.25f.). Moreover the New Testament writers seem to be aware of the contradictions that their mythology plunges them into. Side by side with the notion of

110

demons and cosmic forces of evil, which are presumably irresistible, there is the clear call of Jesus to personal decision and action: 'Follow me'.

This argument leads to the question: how is the gospel to be stated in terms that do not involve mythology at all? This is a hard and perhaps insoluble question because, once Bultmann's point about mythology is taken, it is reasonable to go on to raise fundamental questions concerning all religious language and all reference to God as one who wills and speaks and acts. Bultmann was aware of the problem but was unable to solve it. He did, however, reduce the problem to a minimum by making use of that form of philosophical understanding that was current among his contemporaries on the Continent, that is, existentialism.

Existentialism is not a philosophical system. It is rather a revolt from systems. Negatively, existentialists argue in the following way. Philosophers in the past have tended to take on the role of spectators of the human drama. They have, as it were, sat in the gallery and given a complete account of the play and even the structure of the stage. Their accounts of human life and experience are written with the detachment of someone who is not part of the scene. There is no element of personal participation in what they have to say. The grounds for such an approach are clear. Truth must have a universal quality. It is not a function of one man's limited experience. So the philosopher tries to rise above individual awareness to the level of pure abstraction, above the particular to the universal and the essential.

Such systems, say the existentialists, ignore the crucial factor in human understanding, that is, direct, concrete, personal experience. The individual may accept a system in theory, but there is an element of unreality about it until he decides and acts. In that moment of decision he moves from a world of phantom truth to a world in which true and false have harsh, practical content. Theorizing is one thing, doing is another. Theorizing is dispensable, doing is life itself. So existentialists show little interest in worlds of thought painstakingly constructed by rational argument and much interest in personal action. This seems like a revolt from the classroom, and so it is. Despite the fact that the most ardent existentialists have been

111

intellectuals, despite the fact that, at the end of the day, existentialists are found constructing systems of their own, the movement has always retained an iconoclastic and anti-intellectualist flavour.

How does one interpret the New Testament from an existentialist position? By concentrating on the actual situation of each individual and interpreting the gospel in terms of his choice and actions. The intangible and unseen truths lose their importance. That Jesus lived and died and rose, that he is the Saviour of the world, that God will bring the world to judgement are beside the point. These things belong to the world of theoretical, unlived truth. What matters is whether the individual can encounter the living Christ now, whether he can make the bold step of faith and prove salvation for himself amid the concrete realities of his own existence. If he can, the statement that Jesus is the Saviour of the world becomes a tolerable abstraction reflecting the truths of his own existence. If he cannot, the statement has no substance and no meaning.

The loss of New Testament mythology is thus no loss at all. What matters is that the challenging word of the New Testament should be heard again and that every man should have the opportunity to leave all behind and step out into the new life of the kingdom. This is what happens when the gospel is preached as an existential reality and a man believes.

Man in every generation has been deeply aware of his own immortality. He has immortal longings but no assurance of immortality. He has ideals that remain unfulfilled. He is alternately elated and frustrated. He grabs at the world's securities only to find that they are no more secure than he. Sooner or later he falls a victim to sickness and to death. He feels it as an outrage and formulates protests in his mind, but to whom can he protest? He is aware that he contributes to his own contradictions and bears some responsibility for them. This is the state of anxiety which, according to biblical mythology, came upon man through the Fall. This is Paul's 'natural man'. This is the common man of modern times.

To such men the New Testament gospel is offered in preaching. It does not speak of what happened long ago. It is not bolstered by logical or historical arguments. It does not propose ideas that can be accepted mentally. In it God confronts man

112

in his heart, in his will, in his concrete experience, and calls for instant decision and action. That is the true force of the Bible. When thus presented to man in preaching as a challenge to action, the Bible comes alive. When, trembling on the brink of decision, man hears the gospel proclaimed, it becomes for him truly historical because a living option stands before him. Only in this situation does the Bible have historical significance and positive meaning.

The act of faith is indeed an act. Man responds to the offer of renewal in the gospel by turning hopefully to the new life of faith and love which has no grounding in the logic of this world. So he becomes a new creature, and his faith is constantly renewed by divine offer and acceptance in every practical situation that he ever meets.

The disappearance of the intellectual superstructure of Christianity leads many to ask how this can be regarded as a Christian process at all. The answer of Bultmann, the Christian existentialist, is emphatic. What we have just described *is* the Christian faith. There is no other. Man can do nothing to save himself. Release is made possible by the free gift of God mediated in preaching. The Word calls man to new life. That is the heart of the matter. To express the faith in any other way is to fall back into the primal heresy of replacing faith with works, albeit in this case the intellectual work of subscribing to articles of belief.

Thus the existentialists, who, in terms of New Testament criticism, appear as the greatest of radicals, prove themselves to be defenders of the doctrine of justification by faith. As long as faith is associated with accepting propositions set in a mythological framework and belonging to a history that is long since past—propositions, that is to say, that are 'unlived' by the believer, such as 'Jesus ascended into heaven'—so long will faith be confused with works and even with superstition. Only when all that strain is gone and God confronts the seeker with the offer of grace is the gospel made clear.

None the less, existentialist interpretation of the Bible is making little impression in Britain. It may be that people cling to the security that the biblical world-view seems to give. It may be that the subjectivity of the approach reveals its ultimate inadequacy. It may be that, in the end, universal truth is not irrelevant. Perhaps the best conclusion is that this form of interpretation provides a warning against bogus security disguised as faith and against the tendency to see the search for faith as an intellectual game. It provides also a stimulus to reading the Bible in terms of the concrete facts of life. It does not provide a neatly packaged account of biblical teaching, or a three-point method of interpretation for all to use. Interpretation, the existentialists would say, is too serious for that. The Bible is for living.

17

CONCLUSION

We have now taken a good look at some of the issues involved in biblical interpretation and at different approaches to the problem of resolving them. None the less many readers may feel that none of the approaches entirely satisfies them. This is not surprising. We have discussed four or five broad areas, but even so, few readers will want to identify themselves completely with one of them. Thoughtful people rebel against classification; they are not given to saying, 'I am a liberal', 'I follow Bultmann', 'I go with Barth'.

As far as biblical interpretation goes this refusal to be labelled is well advised. The subject is one of immense complexity. It bears on the whole field of belief and practice. It has to be integrated with so many other departments of theology that to settle for being a liberal or a fundamentalist without qualification is really to opt out of the struggle. Most readers will find virtues in every approach and will try to profit from them all as they press on with the patient and serious task of working out their own attitude to the Bible, their own methods of understanding it and their own theological convictions.

There is, perhaps, another reason why readers hesitate before espousing one of these approaches to the exclusion of the others. It is not simply that interpretation is a complicated task but that we are complicated people. We who interpret are believers. We must be, or we would be content to leave the Bible alone, or to read it for pleasure, or to subject it to our own judgement. We believe in the Bible. That means that we encounter it on different occasions and in many different contexts. Each encounter evokes a response, but the responses vary.

Interpretation suggests a cool, intellectual enterprise, and so it is. Interpretation, for all of us, must be a strict academic study. But we do not spend all our time at desks. We read the Bible for private devotion. We discuss it with groups of like-minded people. We see it dramatized, we hear it sung. Above all we meet it in worship when it is ceremonially honoured and read and expounded. These other contexts are not to be set over against the academic process, but no one will deny that there is a difference of mood between them. There is no opposition between a careful and studious interpretation of the incident in 1 Kings 18 where Elijah clashes with the prophets of Baal and listening to the Mendelssohn oratorio, but as personal experiences they differ profoundly. Happy the man who can be enriched by both. At the end of the day, however, it will be difficult for him to measure and assess the various impressions that the biblical words have made on him and work them all into a system. Life is more complicated than that, and the Bible, as we have said, is for living.

The believer knows that the Bible is able to meet him at every point of his experience, whether he is consciously interpreting or not. This is its glory and the ground of its uniqueness. No method and no system must be allowed to impede that process. No book on interpretation succeeds if it encourages readers to set limits to the Bible and to try to bring it under their control. For the believer knows that, in the last resort, the Bible is only a medium. On one side stands the God who speaks, on the other the man of faith who hears and believes and acts. It is not given to any book, simple or profound, to furnish the full script of that dialogue.

FOR FURTHER READING

Barr, J., *Old and New in Interpretation*. S.C.M. Press 1966.

Barr, J., *The Bible in the Modern World*. S.C.M. Press 1973.

Barth, K., *The Doctrine of the Word of God: Prolegomena to Church Dogmatics*. T. and T. Clark 1936.

Blackman, E. C., *Biblical Interpretation: the Old Difficulties and the New Opportunity*. Independent Press 1957.

Braaten, C. E., *New Directions in Theology Today, vol. 2: History and Hermeneutics*. Lutterworth 1968.

Bright, J., *The Authority of the Old Testament*. S.C.M. Press 1967.

Bultmann, R., *Jesus Christ and Mythology*. S.C.M. Press 1960.

Burthchael, J. T., *Catholic Theories of Biblical Inspiration since 1810: a Review and Critique*. Cambridge University Press 1969.

Cambridge History of the Bible

    Vol. 1: Ackroyd, P. R. and Evans, C. F., ed., *From the Beginnings to Jerome*. Cambridge University Press 1970.

    Vol. 2: Lampe, G. W. H., ed., *The West from the Fathers to the Reformation*. Cambridge University Press 1969.

    Vol. 3: Greenslade, S. L., ed., *The West from the Reformation to the Present Day*. Cambridge University Press 1963.

van Daalen, D. H., *The Real Resurrection*. Collins 1972.

Davidson, R. and Leaney, A. R. C., *The Pelican Guide to Modern Theology vol. 3: Biblical Criticism*. Pelican 1970.

Dodd, C. H., *The Authority of the Bible*. Fontana 1960.

Dodd, C. H., *The Bible Today*. Cambridge University Press 1947.

Dugmore, C. W., ed., *The Interpretation of the Bible*. 1944.

Evans, C. F., *Is 'Holy Scripture' Christian?* S.C.M. Press 1971.

Fuller, R. H., *Interpreting the Miracles.* S.C.M. Press 1963.

Fuller, R. H., *The New Testament in Current Study.* S.C.M. Press 1963.

Grant, R. M., *A Short History of the Interpretation of the Bible.* Black 1948 (revised 1965).

Hanson, A., ed., *Vindications: Essays on the Historical Basis of Christianity.* S.C.M. Press 1966.

Henry, C. F. H., ed., *Revelation and the Bible: Contemporary Evangelical Thought.* Tyndale Press 1959.

Keller, E. and M.-L., *Miracles in Dispute: A Continuing Debate.* S.C.M. Press 1969.

Leon-Dufour, X., *The Gospels and the Jesus of History.* Fontana 1970.

Lindars, B., *New Testament Apologetic.* S.C.M. Press 1961.

McArthur, H. K., ed., *In Search of the Historical Jesus.* S.P.C.K. 1969.

Mackie, A., trs., *The Bible Speaks Again: A Guide from Holland.* S.C.M. Press 1969.

Neil, W., *The Rediscovery of the Bible.* Hodder 1954.

Neill, S., *The Interpretation of the New Testament 1861-1961.* Oxford University Press 1964 (paper 1966).

Nineham, D. E., ed., *The Church's Use of the Bible.* S.P.C.K. 1963.

Reid, J. K. S., *The Authority of Scripture: A study of the Reformation and Post-Reformation Understanding of the Bible.* Methuen 1957.

Richardson, A., *The Bible in the Age of Science.* S.C.M. Press 1961.

Smalley, B., *The Study of the Bible in the Middle Ages.* Blackwell 1941 (2nd edn 1952).

Vawter, B., *Biblical Inspiration.* Hutchinson 1972.

Some of these books are out of print, but they can be found in libraries. Some older books are included as illustrations of the outlook of their period.

INDEX

Abraham, 41, 57, 67, 93
Adam, 42, 69-70, 93
Alexandria, 67-9
allegory, 5, 64-72, 86
Antioch, 70
apocalyptic, 33, 104
Apocrypha, 10, 40, 51-2
Apollos, 95
Aquinas, 70
Aramaic, 13, 35
Aristeas, letter of, 67
Aristobulus, 67
Athanasius, 53
Augustine, 51, 70-1, 84

Babylon, 15, 65
Baptists, 10
Barrett, C. K., 69
Barth, K., 11, 105, 115
Battle Abbey, 19
Beth-horon, 25
Bethlehem, 27
Bezalel, 44
Blacker, C., 108
Bodily Assumption, 84
Boston Tea Party, 19
Bruce, F. F., 3
Bultmann, R., 106-115

Calvin, J., 81, 89-96
Carmel, 25
Carthage, 53, 78
Charles, R. H., 40, 67
Chaucer, 6
Christian Science, 10, 75
Christology, 7, 30, 61, 102
Clement of Alexandria, 69
Conservative Evangelicals, 89, 92-3
Copernicus, 16
Cornelius, 58
cosmology, 15, 35, 108, 110

Damasus, 53

Danby, H., 51
David, 32, 34, 57, 62
Deuteronomic History, 33
Diaspora, 51
Divine Afflante Spiritu, 78
Dogmatic Constitution on Divine
  Revelation, 77-8

Eddy, Mary Baker, 10, 75
Egypt, 20, 22, 65
Elijah, 26, 116
Eliot, T. S., 72
Elisha, 26
Erasmus, 3-4, 7
Eucharist, 40, 67
Evangelicals, 92, 98-9
exegesis, 6-7, 59, 86-7
existentialism, 106, 111-4
Exodus, 19-22, 26, 91

Fall, 48
Fundamentalist, 89, 92-3, 115

Galileo, 16
Gennesaret, 25
Gnosticism, 52, 109

Harnack, A., 100, 105
Harold, 19
Hastings, battle of, 19
Hatch, E., 68
Hercules, 26
hermeneutics, 6
Herod, 28, 61
Hitler, 47, 61
Homer, 68
Hopkins, Gerard Manley, 72

Immaculate Conception, 84

Jamnia, 51
Jehoiachin, 65
Jehovah's Witnesses, 6, 10, 75
Jericho, 65

Jerome, 10, 51
Jerusalem, 65
Jones, C. M., 108
John, King, 19
Joseph, 61
Josephus, 28, 51
Judaism, 6, 9, 15, 37, 40, 43, 50-2, 57-61, 65, 71, 74-5, 86, 91, 98, 104, 106

Knox, J., 79

Lear, King, 46, 48
Lebanon, 64-5
Leo XIII, 79
literalism, 78, 89-97
Loewe, M., 108
Luther, M., 41, 51, 81, 85-6, 88-90

Magna Carta, 19
Marcion, 52
Mariamne, 27
Mary, 61, 84
Mass, 79
McNeill, J. T., 96
Mendelssohn, 116
Messiah, 38-40, 57-9, 62, 93
Methodists, 10
Mishnah, 51
modernist, 93
Mons, 28
Mormons, 10, 75
Moscow, 71
Moses, 23, 45, 57-8, 67
Muslims, 91
mythology, 5, 13-8, 25-6, 32, 35, 106-14

Nazareth, 57, 62, 103
Nebuchadnezzar, 64, 103
Nuremberg, 47

oral tradition, 20-2, 44-5
Origen, 69-71

parable, 5, 64-6
Passchendaele, 11
Passover, 22
Paul, 7, 14, 16-7, 34-5, 38, 41, 44, 52, 58, 60, 66-7, 74, 86, 93, 95, 103
Pentateuch, 45, 50, 79
Pentecost, 61, 71
Perseus, 26
Peter, 61
Pharaoh, 65
Pharisees, 63
Philo, 68-9

Plato, 95
Priestly History, 33
Prophets, The, 9, 37, 50, 58, 60, 86
Protestants, 6, 10, 54, 83-5, 88-9, 98-100
Providentissimus Deus, 78
Punch, 46

quest of the historical Jesus, 103
Qumran, 53
Qur'an, 91

rationalism, 98
Red Sea, 19, 67
Reformation, 10, 51, 71, 81, 84, 86
Ritschl, A., 104
Roman Catholics, 6, 10, 52, 54, 71, 75-80, 83, 86, 98, 106
romanticism, 98
Rome, 28
Russell, Charles Taze, 10, 75
Russia, 71

Samson, 43-44
Schleiermacher, 98
Septuagint, 51
Sheol, 61, 108
sola scriptura, 84
Son of Man, 7, 104
Smith, Joseph, 10, 75
Spiritus Paraclitus, 78
Stalin, 71
Suffering Servant, 104
symbolism, 5, 14-7, 64, 66, 70

Tertullian, 78
Thirty-nine Articles, 51, 84
Titans, 15
Tobolsk, 71
Torah, 9, 34, 37, 40, 50, 54, 57-61, 63-4, 67, 71, 74, 91
tradition, 76-8, 84
Trent, Council of, 51, 78
typology, 42, 67, 86

Vatican, II 77-8
Verdun, 11
Victoria, Queen, 100
Virgin Mary, 84

Wesley, Charles, 72
Wimbledon, 46
Wisdom literature, 33
Writings, The, 9, 37, 50, 58

Zagreus, 15
Zedekiah, 65

120